HONOUR
AND CARE
for PARENTS

DR. SIMEON MEREMOTH

HONOUR AND CARE FOR PARENTS
Dr. Simeon Onyema Meremoth

Copyright © 2020

ISBN 978-978-37467-8-7

Published in Nigeria by
Honour & Care International

For further information or permission, address:
Honour & Care International
18, Akinwale Street,
Off Thomas Salako Street,
Ogba Lagos.
Tel: 08023024692, 08065085620,
E-mail: honourandcare1@yahoo.com

Table of Contents

DEDICATION

To our daughter Victory Chiamaka & Our Son
Reuben Idieli for their special day.

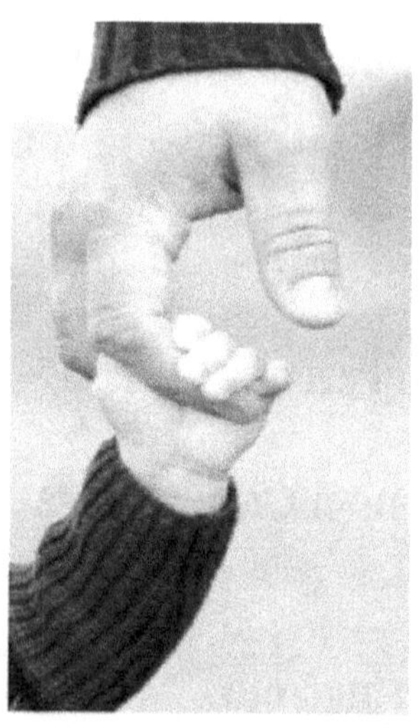

**Any man can be a father,
but it takes someone
bold and courageous
to be a dad**

**...it takes someone
with a heart of rose,
always open, always
loving to be a mother**

ACKNOWLEDGMENT

I wish to express my profound gratitude to all the great people who worked tirelessly to make this book possible.

I want to specially mention Chief (Dr) Mrs. Edna Nze (Ada Imo) Executive Director, Edysmart Nigeria Ltd and High Chief Elkanah O. Mowarin, Executive Chairman / C.E.O, E.O.M Communications Group for great editorial work.

Lastly to my wife, Mrs Precious Meremoth and our lovely children Victory, Francess. Livingseed, HolyHill and Doreen.

You are simply the best.

DR. JOHN OLUSHOLA OJO JP @ 85.

Honour and Care for parents, can be likened to a farmer who goes to farm to plant seeds with the hope of harvest in future. The farmer's seed will germinate, grow and bear fruits. You are that farmer. Your actions and inactions towards your parents are the seeds. You will grow old by the grace of God. Congratulations.

However, the same honour, care, dishonour or carelessness you plant in the lives of your parents today, will become harvest, as you go to the farm at old age. The interesting aspect of seed sowing is that, the harvest is always greater than the seed. The harvest is usually multiplied.

Have you ever sat down to count the harvest of a seed of maize? Today's actions and inactions towards your parents, are seeds of tomorrow's harvest. Please, honour and care for your parents.

I strongly recommend that parents, potential parents and youths, grab copies of this book to read and give as gift to friends, to avert the danger of had I known in future.

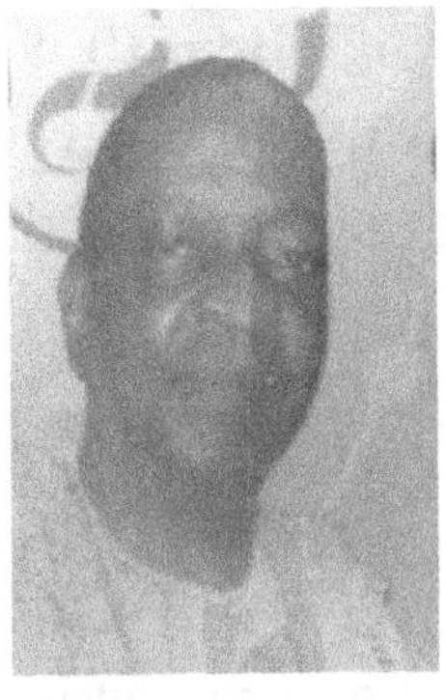

Dr. John Olushola Ojo (JP)
Chairman,
Christ Apostolic Church.
Odi-Ajaye Zone,
Ogba, Lagos.

REV. J.S.A. OLADELE @ 81

The most important personalities in one's life are his or her parents; they are the major avenue through which our being on earth is made possible, without them you wouldn't have existed. Indeed, the root meaning of the word 'parent' is "to cause to be", to happen, or caused to come into".

From the above, it implies that you owe your existence to your parents, and that they are partly what you become. This is true because you derive your gene and some of your character traits from them. These character traits which determines your behavior are the major contributors to your life's success story.

The other point is the nurture you receive from them before you attain the age of accountability. It is said that your nurture determines your nature. Therefore, the result you get in life is traceable to the direct nurture you received from your parents. Therefore, nurture is the foundation seed of whatever you become in life. When this seed planted in you, germinates and grows, it yields increased harvest of greatness and wealth. Parents as the sowers of the seed, must be the first partakers of the harvest.

"The husbandman that laboureth must be first partaker of the fruits

2 Timothy 2:6

This scripture places a moral responsibility over everyone to allow parents reap what they sowed.

The next point is a command. Everyone that wants good life must adhere to it, in other to provoke God's blessing.

"Honour your father and mother; which is the first commandment with a promise; That it may be well with you and you may live long on the earth.

Ephesians 6:2-3

The word "honour" means "fix a valuation upon or cost placed upon a thing based on its value, while care is to be favourably disposed towards someone; or concern based on your understanding of one's need.

The value you attach to your parents should be high, because the more valuable they are to you, the more you endeavour to preserve, and protect them. This commandment has its attendance benefits... *"That it will go well with you and you may live long on the earth"*.

Rev. J.S.A. OLADELE.
GENERAL OVERSEER,
CITY OF THE LORD CHURCH,
LAGOS, NIGERIA.

KATO CHRISTIANA (MRS) @ 66

You honour your parents when you hold them in high esteem, respect them, applaud their values and make them yours. Pass on their Godly teachings and live by their wisdom. Celebrate them and rejoice in their victories, sorrow alongside them, receive their comfort and share yours with them.

When you honour your parents, you live in obedience to God's commandment, the only one with a promise. Trusting in God alone, you receive the promise of a well-lived life, so your children may in turn honour you. I endorse this book as a must read for every home.

KATO CHRISTIANA (MRS)
LOKOJA, NIGERIA.

BISHOP DUNCAN PHILIP @ 58

In Apostle Paul's letter to the Ephesians 6:1-2, he stated clearly, that children obey and honour their spiritual and biological parents. It is a commandment and unconditional obligation. Until you humble yourself, you cannot honour your parents. Obedience is the seed of humility that births dignity and honour.

We first learn to obey our parents before honouring them. We cannot honour and care for our parents, until we first learn to obey them as commanded. **(Psalm 25:9, Philipians 2:5-12)**

Honour is the master key to enjoy the breast milk of our parents, which is their blessing to us. Discover more of God's plan for your life in this great book

Bishop Duncan Philip,
General Overseer,
Word of Love Freedom Ministries,
(a.k.a Freedom Chapel)Worldwide,
Lagos, Nigeria.
+234-8186012111

JOHN K. AMAH, PhD @ 58

The scriptures in Exodus 20:12 says, "Honour your father and mother, that your days may be long upon the land which the Lord your God is giving you." This is one of the core values that is taught to every Jewish child. There is a promise of longevity and prosperity attached to that practice.

All over the world today, the Jews remain the richest individuals. I implore every son and daughter to, take the issue of honour and care for parents seriously. Whether your parents treated you well as a child or not, trained you in higher institution or not, you owe them honour and care.

If you honour and care for your parents, the almighty God will play His part by prospering and giving you long life. I hereby, endorse this book.

REVD. JOHN K. AMAH, PhD
DISTRICT SUPERINTENDENT,
SANGO (FAVOURED) DISTRICT,
ASSEMBLIES OF GOD, NIGERIA.
dramah1962@yahoo.com

JOHN K. AMAH, PhD @ 58

The scriptures in Exodus 20:12 says, "Honour your father and mother, that your days may be long upon the land which the Lord your God is giving you." This is one of the core values that is taught to every Jewish child. There is a promise of longevity and prosperity attached to that practice.

All over the world today, the Jews remain the richest individuals. I implore every son and daughter to, take the issue of honour and care for parents seriously. Whether your parents treated you well as a child or not, trained you in higher institution or not, you owe them honour and care.

If you honour and care for your parents, the almighty God will play His part by prospering and giving you long life. I hereby, endorse this book.

REVD. JOHN K. AMAH, PhD
DISTRICT SUPERINTENDENT,
SANGO (FAVOURED) DISTRICT,
ASSEMBLIES OF GOD, NIGERIA.
dramah1962@yahoo.com

APOSTLE MARTIN ALLIES @ 77.

Your parents, biological and spiritual, are qualified for your obedience, honour and care. It is the will of God, that children obey their parents in the Lord. It is right before God and Man, that sons and daughters obey, honour and care for their parents in righteousness.

As long as the instructions and advice of parents are Godly, we are commanded to obey them. Those who obey their parents, receive the promises of wellness and longevity here on earth. Your parents, biological and spiritual, are qualified for your obedience, honour and care.

Parents are encouraged to avoid toxic lifestyles that makes them self centred, thereby, undermining the interest of their children. it is this toxicity that leads to provocations.

However, sons and daughters are encouraged to do their best to overcome the toxicity of such parents, bearing in mind that, honour and care for parents, is like the divine law of sowing and reaping. (See

Ephesians 6:1-4) I hereby, recommend this book to all.

Apostle Martin Allies,
General Overseer,
Ray of Hope Church,
Boksburg, South Africa.

PROF. RONNIE MOODLEY @ 66

Honor and Care should not be a Word or Action to any person because of Old Age but rather an Action of Respect & Love always from a Son's or Daughter's Spirit.

To Honor alone means to protect you even when you are unaware of it. An action of a Joshua to a Moses that even when you as a Son or Daughter is unaware. The Reward from God is to Bless You as a Son or Daughter with the Legacy of Continuing with your Parents Journey to a New Destination.

When a Daughter or Son can anoint the Feet that preached & Brings Great Messages that Transforms lives as Mary did is symbolic of Appreciating The Foot Prints of the Master.

Today I salute all Sons & Daughters for Honoring the Parents with Respect & Love. The Baton is never long but be EXPECTANT for the Hand of the Lord to pass it on to you like Elisha was to Elijah and Joshua was to Moses & as Jesus Our Lord Sent the Daughter at the Well to be the 1st Evangelist. Your Rewards are

Great and Mighty from the Lord. I recommend this book. Bless You All.

Professor Ronnie Moodley
Overseer Faith Ministry Int'l
Dean Faith Bible College
Johannesburg, South Africa

VICTORIA NWACHINEMERE UGBOAJA @ 56

Truly, aging is a fact of life here on earth. One of the times to bestow love and care to parents should be at old age.

One sure way of honouring parents is to maintain our respect for them, by way of taking care of them at old age.

This is what we do here in Abundant Grace Care Homes, by helping to nurse and care for the elderly parents, who have served, retired and now need care and support extended to them.

This act of love goes a long way in extending the life span of parents and ensuring that they happily, complete their respective days here on earth.

When we do this, we build treasures of future harvest for our own times of old age, also receive the blessings of our parents, as the leadership mantle is passed on to us.

God is pleased, when we honour and care for our parents.

VICTORIA NWACHINEMERE UGBOAJA, (MSc. Nursing)
HOUSTON TEXAS,
USA.

DR. SIMEON & PRECIOUS MEREMOTH
DURING THEIR WEDDING, 1989

THE HONOURABLE LIFE: The choice to live a life, that is characterized by high moral standards like honesty, fairness, integrity and reverence of God in our thoughts, beliefs and behaviour is considered honourable, distinguished and virtuous. Any person who exhibits the above traits should be accorded great respect. Honour is the source of credit or distinction in any pursuit in life.

THE GREAT CHALLENGE: It is on record however, that our endless desire and pursuit for wealth, recognition, dominion, lordship, drug addiction and reign over others rob us of our honour, integrity and fear of God on a daily basis. As we get deeply involved in satanic deception of drugs, culture, morality and self-indulgence, we end up in dishonor and lose our directions in life.

Many desires to be known and addressed as honourable whereas, in reality their lifestyles and characteristics are totally dishonourable and full of petty stuff. Honourable people are not supposed to mismanage, steal or embezzle funds entrusted in their care.

They are expected to speak to the truth as men and women of honour. They have no business with thugs, killings, lootings and conversion of public properties to their names. They stand for fairness, integrity, honesty and exemplary leadership.

Our quest for political, occultic and worldly powers at all cost has left us with names our children cannot attempt to present or bear anywhere for lack of merit and integrity.

So many are pleased to continue to labour to acquire ill-gotten wealth that their children are not ready to inherit after them. We tend to deceive ourselves by wearing black garments to rob in the secret only to appear in the public with white garments.

The honourable life is an internal control to revealing our full potentials in life as sincere, mature and moral human beings here on earth.

HOW TO LIVE HONOURABLY: To live honourably is to reverence God, do our best in all aspects of daily living with courage, integrity, purpose and dignity. Moreover, it means pursuit of excellence in all that we do in life and to make the most use of our life and time in the light of God's word, Saying the right thing, and always standing for the right thing and for the reason.

In pursuit of honourable living, there is need to make the most use of opportunities in life, to enable you make the most impact here on earth. Maximize your life and abilities by doing all the good you can. Give the very best you can offer to make most use of your talents, opportunities and influence in your environment. When you live honourably you make your life a masterpiece, sign your name to everything good and abstain from everything bad.

If truly you want to be remembered, live with honour and you shall be remembered even when you are no more.

1
HONOUR YOUR PARENTS:

Now that you have known what honourable life is and how to live honourably, the first step of showing respect to your parents, should be pursuit of honourable living. Decide to fear God and pursue those values that will give your parents joy, respect, high esteem before God and men. Let your actions and inactions demonstrate your inward assessment of how highly you esteem them and how much their parentage impacted your life. Your business, career and the events that surround your life should be free from shame. Your life should bring them respect before men and women in the land.

The news about you should lighten and not darken their faces before the public. Your desires, aspirations and pursuits in life should bring honour to them wherever they go. The news of your fear of God should refresh their bones and marrows. The breaking news of your breakthroughs and accomplishments in life should stand them out in the society. May the aroma of your good news and lifestyle lift up their heads wherever they are introduced. May people draw closer and associate with them because of your testimonial.

You honour your parents when your decisions and actions in life showcase wisdom and understanding of properly trained son or daughter. Your life should radiate honour and not dishonour. The news about you should give your parents joy and not heartache.

Honour them with your love, obedience and exemplary lifestyle at home and abroad. Honour them with listening ears to their Godly advice and suggestions. Honour them with pursuit of genuine means of livelihood and not fraudulent ostentation and destructive actions.

Let them see the hope of generation continuity through you while they are still alive. Let your love for God and humanity give them joy.

You honour your parents by staying away from drugs and other criminal actions that will destroy the goodwill of the family and rubbish their achievements in life.

When you honour your parents you honour God. That is why God attaches so much importance to it with a promise of longevity. You honour your parents each time you run away from actions that dishonour God in your life. Let God be glorified in your life.

WHO IS A PARENT?

A parent is one's Father or mother. The duo is referred to as parents. Your parents are responsible for your co-creation. In the beginning, God created one man and woman and transferred the power to procreate through fruitfulness to man and woman. Every human has a father and mother otherwise known as parents. They procreated you in their own image in fulfillment of God's command to be fruitful and multiply.

Just like God said to the son Jesus Christ, and the Holy Spirit:

"Let us make man in our own Image, after our likeness, and let them have dominion over the fish of

the sea, and over the fowl of the air, and over the cattle, and over all the earth, and over every creeping thing that creepeth upon the earth" **(Genesis 1:26)**

In the same manner your father and mother agreed to co - create you in their own image and likeness. The assignment is carried out by the agreement of the duo through submission to one another, whether knowingly or unknowingly. They are instrumental to your being conceived and delivered at the ninth month.

God desires that we love, honour and care for our parents. Jesus Christ, our Saviour and Lord is our perfect example on how to love our parents. Even at the point of death, He still loved and cherished His earthly mother Mary. He made sure that the future of His mother was secured, by handing her over to the one He loved. Hear Him;

26. When Jesus therefore saw His mother, and the disciple standing by, whom He loved, He said unto His mother, woman behold thy son!

27. Then said He to the disciple, Behold thy mother! And from that hour that disciple took her unto his own home. **John 19:26-27**

Wherever your parents are, you are expected to honour and care for them in life. It is God's will that your parents live together as one and under one roof as they raise Children, but sometimes, it does not work out as planned.

However, whether they live together after your birth or not you are expected to know your parents, reach out to them as they reach out to you. Love, honour and care for them for life.

WHAT IS HONOUR?

Honour is to be respectful in your actions and words to your parents and a demonstration of an inward attitude of high esteem for whom and what they are and represent to you. It is to revere, price or value one highly. God has placed so much premium on the issue of honour for your parents that He made it the first commandment with a promise attached to its obedience.

God expects us to place higher priority to honour and care for our parents. Refusing to honour and care for your parents is not only suicidal, it is guaranteed by God to lead to your destruction, and truncate your destiny here on earth.

THE IMPORTANCE OF HONOUR

Let's look at some of the reasons why so much emphasizes have been placed on honour for parents. In the beginning, God gave this commandment to His children through Moses.

Honour your father and thy mother that thy days may be long upon the land which the Lord thy God gives thee. **Exodus 20 :12**

Apostle Paul, took up the issue in his letter to the Ephesians in chapter six verse two and three and amplified the Exodus chapter twenty verse twelve to include the wellness or prosperity of body soul and Spirit.

"Honour thy father and mother; which is the first commandment with promise. That it may be well

for living. What a sweet mother! Your endless cry day and night kept your mother sleepless. Your refusal to eat made her restless and forget to eat.

Now you can do so many things on your own, but don't forget that your parents at a time, did all you are doing now for you. Here are some major reasons for God's position on honour and care for parents.

THEY CONCEIVED AND DELIVERED YOU:

The agreement of your father and mother to meet led to your conception and delivery. If they had not agreed on having you at the time you were conceived, they wouldn't have had you. They had the satanic option of aborting your conception.

However, through the fear of God, they allowed your development from day one to ninth month when you were born. That singular reason calls for your appreciation and honour for your parents. Think of the love that propelled a mother's strength to carry you in the womb for nine (9) Months

Your delivery was another wonderful aspect of your coming. Your mother had the option of bringing you out still, but she endured the labour pain and pushed you out alive. That's inestimable love from a great mother. You are not a biological accident. You are a well thought out and greatly cherished will of your parents.

You didn't just come into the world. Your parents showed you the way. The role God played in bringing you into the world was supernatural and it could only become natural with the cooperation of your father and mother. You owe them all the honour and care you can afford in life.

Yes, you may cease to be their child at a time, but you remain their son or daughter for life. Marriage only moves you up from childhood to sonship or daughterhood and there you live for life and procreate children, who later become sons and daughter to take over from you. So, for life you are somebody's son or daughter.

The duo who through thoughtful imagination or expression say, *"Come let us raise children in our own image and likeness are called Parents"* Please, honour and care for them as long as they live.

Don't tell me that you cannot honour and care for your parents because they told you that they are now witches and wizards. Don't tell me how wicked and frustrating they have been. Don't even accept the demonic insinuations that they want to kill you, because they had ample time to kill you before now, and they never did it. Your claim that you are now light and they are darkness cannot hold water. Shine your light in darkness and the light will expose any darkness.

Sometimes, what we call wickedness in the lives of parents may be the result of severe challenging situation in their lives at that time. Their wicked action may have been God's master - minded plan unknown to any mankind, to save your life.

Some years back, one of the men in our ministry, who had four (4) children already at the time, rushed to my house early morning,and announced that he found, a day-old baby in the gutter on his way to work. He wanted to ask me what to do. I told him to go pick up the baby. He picked up the baby and returned to me.

I asked him to go to the police and make an entry that he picked up a day-old baby boy. He did and the police took note and referred him to Welfare Department. The Welfare Department asked him, if he has interest in keeping and training the boy? He answered positive. That was all that the welfare authorities needed from him. They asked him to go with the baby.

Permit me to say here, that the boy is growing up in wisdom, stature and status, competing favourably in academics with the rest children of the man.

As I write this book, the young boy does not know his biological parents. The man and I do not also know who the authors of this brilliant boy are, but God knows.

Now, if this boy whose identity is withheld, par adventure meets the mother. What will be your expected or suggested reaction of the boy towards the mother? Just keep your answer to yourself.

My interest is that the gutter was the best place for the boy to be at that point in time. Sometimes, this innocent boy could be a product of lust of the flesh of young students or even jobless youths. Before you conclude on the above, reflect on this:
In 1986, I had an apartment in another part of the town in Lagos State, Nigeria. One day I got up to use the toilet that I shared with other tenants in the yard, only to see a premature baby flushed into the toilet. That same day, I abandoned that apartment. I was only three months old in that yard. I believe that baby was aborted by human.

One conceived, delivered and threw into the gutter. The other aborted at about four months or so. Where are you Cain? What's your stand Abel? Did you know how many times the devil suggested to your parents to abort you? Did you know how many people that talked your parents into offloading you? Please, pause and rethink on the love, care and protection your parents provided for you and learn to honour and care for them, and it shall be well with you in the land of the living.

THEY WERE THE FIRST TO SHELTER YOU:

How often young men and women forget that their parents were the first to provide them with accommodation. Parents were the first to shelter you. Your first room was your mother's womb.

They pointed you to where you returned to each day you left the house, for so many years. Today you read and hear stories that look like movies, where sons and daughters ask their parents to move out of their houses as if any of them can ever accommodate his or her parents the number of years or length of time their parents accommodated him or her.

From your parent's thatch house, they gave you comfort in secondary school by paying for your hostel accommodation. Now you are a graduate, working and living in a posh house, while your parents in the village are still in that same house where they sacrificed to give you shelter in college.

Are your parents born to live in penury? Why did they give you the name Hope? Why were you called [The future is greater?] Why should that old house be leaking while your dog's house is air-conditioned? Why should your parents be sleeping on mat while your pussy cat sleeps on rug? Why did they name you [Wealth is ahead] at birth?

Have you checked out your name? Do you know what was the condition of things at that time that warranted their choice of your name?

Whereas you are spending time abroad with choice personalities in choice places, your parents' blood pressure jumps up whenever there is sign of an impending rainfall. With the reduced life expectancy all over the world, due to sin and pollution, when will your parents harvest their expectation of your arrival and support in life? Would you be proud to take your friends and colleagues to your parent's house at home? What's on your mind? Why spend millions in burying a parent that never exited from suffering all the days of his or her life? Why buy a golden casket to bury a parent who never ate with a silver spoon?

THEY PROVIDED YOUR COVERING: No matter how wealthy you are today; you shouldn't forget that your parents provided the first clothes you wore. Your parents clothed you the moment you were born. Just like God clothed Adam and Eve.

YOUR PARENTS FED YOU:

You had the great privilege of surviving hunger because your parents were handy to feed you as at when due. Your first restaurant was your mother's kitchen. That you had unwanted food does not mean that many children never died of malnutrition.

I am thankful to my parents for feeding me from day one to such a time I could responsibly feed myself. Their act of benevolence has helped me to achieve a sterling health of not rising and falling in health as a result of lack of care. The one that gave you food to eat at the time of hunger enabled you to face the next journey to your breakthrough in life. Have you ever paused to appreciate God for your parents? Did you know that some parents served others in order to put food on the table? Did you know that some parents were subjected to abuses to feed their children? Some parents temporarily disobeyed their conscience to save their children from hunger.

Have you asked your parents how they managed to give you the best food when you were born? Many parents went to bed empty stomach while their children had the only meal. Sometimes they declined the offer of dinner because of your breakfast.

I witnessed Mama eat less so I could have something to eat in the morning. When I asked her why, she told me that her mother taught her to place more emphasis on breakfast than dinner. She further explained to me that breakfast is the most important meal. She will always support it with her song: "ori riforomu ututu, Anyasi ma sukoro ba? (that song is in my language [Igbo] and it means: "whoever eats should reserve breakfast for me while I go empty stomach to bed".

I was born into royalty but two factors threw me into poverty. One was the Nigerian soldiers and their war against innocent civilians during the civil war. The war took away my father's job at the Modern Ceramics industries ltd, Umuahia, Abia State. Nigeria.

The same war drove me away from my village to Ikeduru, Imo State, Nigeria, where I wandered in search of abandoned cassava, cocoyam and animals for meat.

The second point was that I returned to a homeless place, the Nigerian soldiers having burnt my father's house. According to them, the enemies of progress, hung the uniform of a Biafran soldier in our house, and that was enough for the mindless soldiers to destroy a house built by my father with his savings.

Having lost my father at the wake of the civil War, precisely in 1967, I returned to a homeless place with my mother and brothers, my senior sisters having been married out already. On return we had no house to live, no father, nothing in the barn as the soldiers had turned to locusts on our barn stock. The rest is story you can tell.

I know what food meant as I reflect on the Nigerian civil war. So if you are alive today, appreciate God for the efforts of your parents. Dear God, I thank you for my parents of blessed memory.

THEY WERE YOUR TEACHERS:
Let him that is taught in the word communicate unto him that teacheth in all good things.
Galatians 6:6

Though this scripture is often directed to spiritual parents, I strongly believe that it has a lot to do with our biological parents too. They were our first teachers. Parents are usually the ones that undertake the business of teaching to speak, sing, greet, pray and read the bible before we find our way to secular schools. They deserve all the good things we can afford to give to them.

YOUR PARENTS EDUCATED YOU
Thank God for making it possible for your parents to send you to college/ University. Your first teacher was your mother. Your first school was your mother's kitchen. However, most people fail to

for the efforts of your parents. Dear God, I thank you for my parents of blessed memory.

THEY WERE YOUR TEACHERS:
Let him that is taught in the word communicate unto him that teacheth in all good things.
Galatians 6:6

Though this scripture is often directed to spiritual parents, I strongly believe that it has a lot to do with our biological parents too. They were our first teachers. Parents are usually the ones that undertake the business of teaching to speak, sing, greet, pray and read the bible before we find our way to secular schools. They deserve all the good things we can afford to give to them.

YOUR PARENTS EDUCATED YOU
Thank God for making it possible for your parents to send you to college/ University. Your first teacher was your mother. Your first school was your mother's kitchen. However, most people fail to

Knowledge=Power=Resources=Authority=Influene =Dominion.

This accounts for the reason an illiterate man on the throne cannot produce resources because he lacks the mental power to create resources. Mental poverty is the worst poverty and it is more dangerous than the other classes of poverty.

It is also wrongful for any leader to think that there is anything like standing still in real life. Those who stand still in the real sense are going backwards. Each time a mentally poorman sits on the throne, the throne becomes lifeless of ideas that can create resources because of the absence of mental power that leads to productivity.

If a child born in 2015, has been sitting or standing at a spot till date, that child is not standing still, but rather going backwards. You are either moving forward or going backwards.

There is no law that permits standing still when there is so much to attend to in a limited time frame in life. One of the greatest things your parents contributed to your life is good education. Please appreciate them for that singular contribution to your journey to dominion. The idea of education is to empower you mentally to face the future confidently.

YOUR PARENTS CARED FOR YOU:

Thank God for a mother's heart, always open and always loving. Your mother was there for you when you cried, needed food, sleep, medication and water for living. What a sweet mother to remember.

Your sleeplessness kept your mother sleepless. Your refusal to eat made her forget or reject her own meal. Think of changing diapers, wiping running noses and hauling you back and forth.

Think of mopping the floor after the milk is spilled for the fourth time during breakfast, lunch or dinner. What of the child running a fever in the middle of the night?

Your parents cared for you from the womb to the time of knowledge of good and evil. Your mother was your first doctor who was readily available with her thermometer to check your body temperature. She was also your best friend at a time in life.

Now, you can do so many things on your own, but don't forget that your parents at a time, did all you are doing on your own now, for you.
Your mother was your first vehicle that hauled you on her back at a time in your life. Oh sweet mother how will I forget you. You deserve more.

YOUR PARENTS TRAINED YOU:

The issue of training cannot be overlooked. Your parents took time to train you in the ways to go in life, so you can live a worthy and acceptable life here on earth. Your first school was your mother's kitchen. The values you showcase in places you go to in life, the good qualities and habits you exhibit are credits to good parental upbringing.

The Bible specifically requires us to train up a child in the way he or she should go and watch him or her manifest that as he or she grows up in life. You may not have access to good education, however, if you have access to good parental upbringing, you can be sure of sitting with great people in life at the fullness of time.

Think of how many things your parents taught you that cannot be obtained as an educational certificate. Think of how many times your parents' impact on you has saved you from danger and destruction. So many of us would have ended up being lazy and unclean if not for the bold assertions of our parents.

Think of areas in life you have challenges today, and your refusal to obey the instructions of your parents at early stages of training in life. Be grateful to God and your parents for showing you the way of godly living and good morals.

YOUR PARENTS PAID YOUR BILLS

Remember to honour and care for your parents because they first honoured your bills from conception, to the time you began picking your bills. The time or duration varies from individual to individual. Some get up early while others wake up late in picking up their own bills. Your parents paid all your bills without fighting or disowning you.

Many of them sold their personal effects, shares in companies and other valuables to pay your bills. I know of parents who pledged their landed properties, while others embarked on outright sale to honour their sons' and daughters' bills. Many parents Sold their gold, and silver apparels to pay the bills of their children. While many borrowed their way through to pay their children' bills. You didn't just get to where you are, somebody was there for you.

THEY LABOURED IN PRAYER AND THE WORD:

For so many years you didn't know how to pray. It was the prayer covering of your parents that kept you going. Even now, most of us are still enjoying the benefits of our parents' prayer covering.

In addition to praying for you, they taught you how to pray during the devotional hours. You might be the best prayer warrior now but your parents were your first teachers on how to pray. Please, learn how to appreciate and celebrate them.

Doors of blessings were opened unto you through the prayers of your parents by the power of the name of Jesus Christ. As you remain connected to your parents at heart and gratitude you will reap more blessings and breakthroughs through their hearty prayers.

YOUR PARENTS TOLERATED YOU: One major reason why you should honour and care for your parents is their level of tolerance. Think of the so many foolish and stupid things you did by way of wrong actions and inactions.

Your first toilet was your mother's laps. You kept your mother's purse restless because of biscuits and sweets. You told her each time she complained that she did not know how much she had in her purse. No matter the amount of meat you are given, you sneaked into mum's kitchen for more. Lying was your stock in trade.

There were cases when you spent hours on errands that are supposed to take just ten (10) minutes because you have to go play or visit a friend first and end up with a story of the money being lost. Can you recall how many times you misbehaved and disobeyed instructions?

You were not willing to do anything even taking care of your own personal effects like clearing your room, washing your clothes and barbing your hair. Washing your own dishes and brushing your teeth was a case. You asked them to leave you alone, that it is your teeth. After all, you now have a bad teeth courtesy of your own disobedience.

They buy things that you need, you carelessly abandon them outside only to report that you are looking for them and so need a replacement.
Sometimes, parents end up with apologies to children where the children are supposed to do otherwise, just to win the children over.

Look at this case: One day, I went to the river to fetch water with a calabash. After a long journey, I stopped on the way to play football. In the course of playing, my calabash was hit by the ball and I wasted the water that I trekked Kilometers to fetch. I also lost the calabash. Meanwhile, my parents were anxiously waiting for my return to have water to use. Having committed multiple offence, I resolved to remain outside, refusing to go home. When the wind of my broken calabash got to my parents, they sourced out water for use. The next thing was for their son to return home, not the broken calabash or water. They embarked on searching for me because it was getting late.

You see, I was the offender yet they tolerated my foolishness and switched on to the issue of my security and safety. You can recall your own story and how many times your parents tolerated your stupidity and foolishness in order to give you a future.

Some of you squandered your school fees and they covered your shame by sourcing out another fund to pay up.

A young man wrote a touching personal confession to me, according to him, he wasted his father's money and estate. His father was sending money from abroad where he was doing odd jobs to establish the family here in Nigeria. The young man gave the father impression that he has invested the money in a small factory they set up, but it was a huge Joke.

One day, he decided to call it quit with life. He wrote his suicide note, fastened the hanger's rope to the hook of the ceiling fan, somehow, he decided to tidy up his room to ensure that his past records are destroyed. While he was clearing his room, one of my books titled "Overtake and be at the top" given to him at a rehabilitation centre, fell off his bag. He took it up and opened to a page that says "it is not over, don't quit". That discouraged him from taking his own life.

At that point, he changed his mind, untied the rope, and believed that it was not over yet. He went back to University of Lagos, Nigeria on his own, and graduated. He promised to refund his father whatever he has wasted of the funds, and to rebuild his estate. He became a changed man and faced life in a new dimension. In all these the father forgave, renewed their relationship and celebrated the son's deliverance from untimely death. What a level of tolerance?

Parents reading this book can write a case study or more of how they were able to tolerate each and every one of their children. God bless our parents in Jesus name. Every son or daughter reading this book can write a better story of his or her wrong actions and inactions towards his or her parents that were tolerated.

THEY ENDURED AND FORGAVE US: Your parents should be greatly remembered for their endurance. That capacity or ability, they showcased over your unpleasant attitude. They had to endure the difficult process of trusting and believing God that you will change one day. They refused to give way that the situation will change for good concerning your attitude towards them and others. You gave them reasons to give up on you.

There were times when you fought them (your parents). There were cases where you caused them serious pain. Some of your actions brought shame, yet they held onto the promises of God to them concerning your conversion, and today you are saved and regenerated.

You don't need Meremoth to remind you to honour and care for such parents, who had such faith in your future and stomached all unfavourable situations that emanated from your carelessness, to ensure that they win you over to honourable living.

Reflect on the days when you joined the gang and lived as a gangster. Everything meant nothing to you but destruction. To you smoking, stealing and taking in any substance, including drugs was the way out. You caused them uncontrolled emotions in private and public life. Yet they held on their love for you. They thought of the cord that bound you together and vowed not to disown you.

This is a typical scenario. Your father writes to remind you that you will blame yourself for every harmful habit you have picked up willingly. You now smoke, drink and sleep in shrine. The future is here already. Your tutors are truly wiser than you. So sad to have a son like you being misled by people you are supposed to lead. A big pity boy.

Then you replied, *"I don't like such text message being sent to me. I am not a kid."* You are not a kid but you depend on your parents. Your bills are fully picked by your parents. You live under their roof. Your future, destiny and life are threatened by the enemy without your knowledge, and your response to your father, is that you are not a kid, So sad.

My beloved reader, if your parents are still alive, pause now and think of what to do to appreciate them. They sincerely gave their best to bringing you to this point of royalty and celebration.

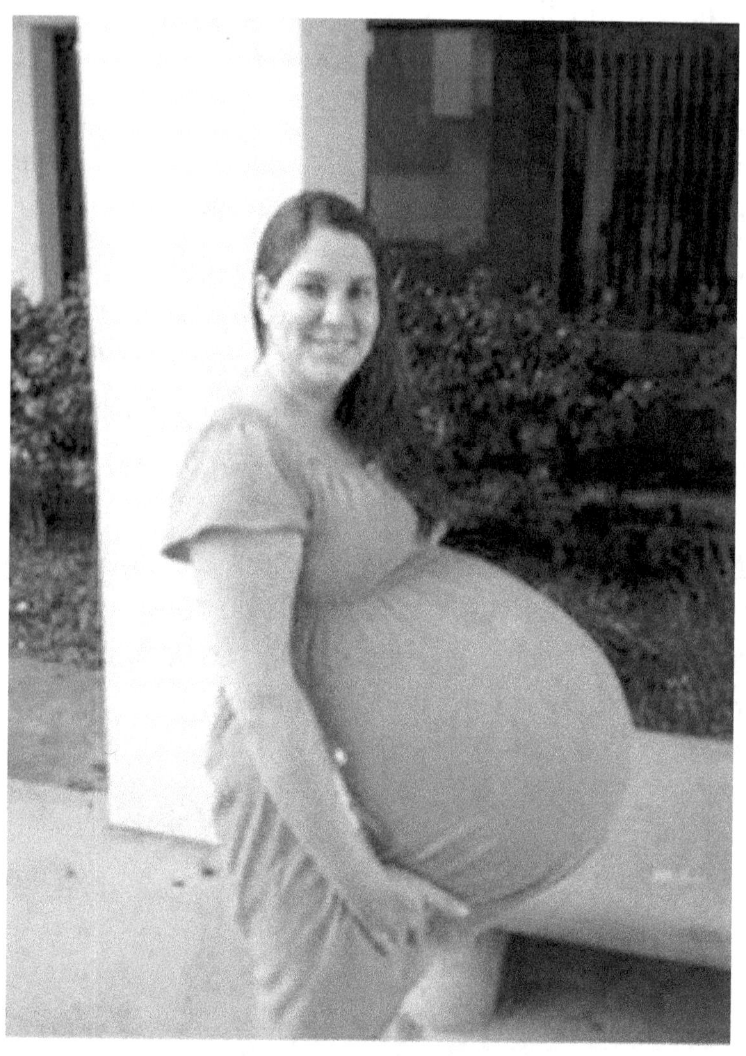

Your mother went through this for you

2
WAYS TO HONOUR YOUR PARENTS:

There are various ways to honour your parents. Here are some of the major ways to express honour to your parents.

BE YOUR FAMILY AMBASSADOR: Every son or daughter is his or her family's ambassador. As an ambassador you are a representative, image maker, a random sample of your family. Your actions, lifestyle, character and values speak volumes of your family.

You are expected to be an ambassador of your family in good behaviour, character, lifestyle of honour and respect for all. Make your parents look good by being a good ambassador.

Don't just appear good in dressing, also appear good in character, attitude and values in life. Let people see your parents in you before they meet your parents.

Your ability to represent your family by way of Godly actions and good behaviour is one of the greatest marks of honour to your parents. Simply be a good son or daughter and men and women will connect to your mom and dad.

OBEY YOUR MOM AND DAD: One of the principal ways to honour your mom and dad is to obey every godly instruction and advice they give to you. God is pleased when you honour your parents with obedience. God also said that it is right to do so. Your parents represent God to you in so many ways here on earth. It is ungodly and rebellious to disobey your parents.

FORGIVE: Offences are bound to occur in every relationship. God extends grace and mercy to us daily, as He grants us forgiveness. The same way He expects us to extend forgiveness freely to our parents whenever offences occur. You cannot afford to live in malice and grudges against your parents.

LOVE THEM AT ALL TIMES: As the years run by, our parents turn to lean on us more than they ever planned. This may lead to a feeling that they are becoming a burden too heavy to bear. That is the beauty of old age. It is the time and season in their lives when your unconditional love should flow towards them in words and actions. As a matter of fact, your love for your mom and dad should be increasing as you get older.

VISIT REGULARLY: Your parents need your warm smile, hearty handshake, a tap on the shoulder or a hug. It speaks volumes of love. This can only be achieved through frequent visits to your parents. They cannot receive the smiles, handshakes, hugs or taps on shoulder or hands, by telephone, video, cards or pictures. You can only deliver them personally, so make out time out of your busy schedule and visit them.

EXPRESS GRATITUDE: Let your parents know that you appreciate what they have been through for you. This will not cost you the money that you don't have. It will only cost you humble words and action. In future you will be privileged to add the monetary and material values in expression of your gratitude.

LISTEN TO YOUR PARENTS STORIES: It is to your own advantage to listen to your parent's stories because this is one of the sure ways of learning. While it provides them with your presence, it affords you the opportunity, if you can slow down, to learn about the past generations, and other experiences your parents have gained in life. Be patient in listening to them. Avoid the habit of walking out on your parents while they tell their stories.

RESPECTFULLY DISAGREE:
There are times when you may vary in your opinion about your parents' stand on a particular issue.

There may be times when you may have to correct your dad and mum, especially if they opt to continue in sin. That's okay, but you must respectfully disagree with hem

Let them have your views respectfully. Don't shout on them or force them to accept your views. Resist the urge to be disrespectful in your manners, actions, thoughts or words. Let your correction or disagreement overflow in love, kindness, patience and respect.

TELL THEM YOUR STORIES:

Your parents are not only interested in telling you their stories, they also want to listen to your stories. They want to know about your future plans and your readiness to seek their opinion. They want to know how you are growing up in life.

Find time to talk to your parents one-on-one, talk to them on phone when you are away from home. In future when you can afford the bill, take them out for dinner, visit for morning tea and family get-together.

SPEAK GOOD OF YOUR PARENTS': No matter the pressure, make it a habit, to remain positive about your parents whenever you are with friends. Get excited over what your parents do to earn a living. Whether mom and dad are school tutors, farmers, civil servants, chauffeurs, traders, or what have you. Be proud of them.

DON'T RIDE ON THEIR INTERESTS OR VALUES: As you grow up and build your own mind on social matters, politics, language, drinking, movies rating, standards and other subject matters of personal interest.

Remember to keep the honour due to your parents along the way. What that means is that, you need to drop your new found habits when you are with them.

For example, if you have taken to smoking or drinking alcohol against their teachings, remember to keep your new habits in the drawer as you visit them and to serve soft drinks when they come to visit you. Avoid getting at loggerheads.

WRITE THEM TRIBUTES:

As you grow up in life, find time to write tribute about your parents. Let them read and know how you feel about them while they are alive. Think of the impeccable morals of your parents, the good character and integrity they taught you and their efforts in teaching you how to be successful in life.Remember their tenacious leadership and family values. Let them know how much you love and cherish their impacts in your life.

HOLIDAY TRIPS:

Whenever it is affordable by you think of surprising your parents with holiday trips to towns or any countries of your choice.

However, if your parents are the type that don't like travelling to other towns and nations, then you are discharged on this subject matter.

ADDITIONAL WAYS OF HONOUR TO YOUR PARENTS:

Honour them with exemplary lifestyle at school, home and abroad. Honour them with pursuit of genuine means of livelihood and not fraudulent means. Avoid ostentation and destructions. Let them see the hope of generational continuity through you while they are still alive.

Let your love for God and humanity give them joy. You honour your parents when your decisions and actions in life showcase wisdom and understanding of properly trained son or daughter. Your life should radiate honour and not dishonour. The news about you should give your parents joy and not heartache.

You honour your parents by staying away from drugs and other criminal actions that will destroy the goodwill of the family and rubbish their achievements in life.

You honour your parents when you honour God and you honour God when you honour your parents because He attaches so much importance to it with a promise of longevity.

To honour your parents is to run away from actions that dishonour God in your life. Give God the glory in your life.

ADDENDUM: The ways and manner to honour your parents are inexhaustible. The scope of this book cannot cover it all. You can therefore add to the above list in your own private study.

CARE FOR YOUR PARENTS

WHAT IS CARE? As stated in page 74 of my book Honour and care for the Man of God (Hard cover) to care is to look after someone or show concern. To give serious attention. In addition to the important issue of honouring your parents, there is need to show concern over their well being.

God expects us to give attention to our parents as he gives us breakthrough in life. We are expected to give serious attention to matters relating to our parents. As parents grow old they need to be cared for and given back the serious attention, passion, and love they taught us over the years. When you care for your parents, you give them confidence to face a vibrant and secured tomorrow.

Caring for your parents is for your own good as it strengthens and refreshes their bones, keeping them joyful and prayerful over all that concerns you and fulfillment of destiny. As you care for your parents, they pour out their love in purposeful prayers for your goodness and prosperity in all that your hand finds to do in life according to God's will.

Caring for your parents keeps you away from curses and groaning as a result of hardship. If your parents spend their days gnashing their teeth in pains and agony, you don't expect all to be well with you. No matter how many times you pray and shout Halleluyah in a day.

Care for your parents gives you access to reward of peace and breakthrough here on earth. When you care for your parents, you demonstrate an inward attitude of high esteem and respect for whom they represent in your life. The circle of life God has given to us through our parents endorses the need for children who have been blessed and cared for by their parents to in turn care for their parents.

THE AGAPE LOVE OF PARENTS:

Think of the sacrificial, free and unequalled love of parents towards their sons and daughters as compared with the love of sons and daughters towards their parents as they grow up.

Aside from onerous task of carrying you in the womb. Parents carry their children on the laps, back, shoulders and hands while working.
How many of us, sons and daughters can reciprocate these wonderful gestures of parents?

Do we have sons and daughters who can be compassionate enough to carry their parents on their hands, laps, back or shoulders at old age? Some of us don't even go near our parents when they are sick or physically challenged.

I have stated earlier on in this book that the circle of life requires that we return the love and care our parents showed to us back to them as we grow up especially at their old age. Pause and reflect on the above issue.

If the challenges that trail old age were to manifest on your parents would you be kind enough to return reasonable percentage of their love and care to them? Can your room become their last room at old age? Can your kitchen become their restaurant at old age as your mother's breast was your first restaurant?

Would you tolerate a little mess from your parents as your mother's laps were your first toilet? Would you willingly become their last teacher at old age as they were your first teachers?

You began schooling in your mother's kitchen. Would you be kind enough to do your research work as a doctor in her kitchen at old age?

Don't forget that they were there for you at infancy. The circle of life requires that you in turn be their last doctor at old age just like your mother was your first doctor, checking your body temperature with her thermometer at infancy?
Are you willing to be their last friend as they were your first friends at cradle? As your mother's back was your first vehicle, can you be exemplary enough to show a little care by allowing your parents to just lean on your body at old age?

What are you ready to do differently with regards to your love to parents after reading this book? It is not enough to sing the song-sweet mother I will not forget you, for suffering for me. How are you willing to practicalize the song?

It is not enough to shout my daddy, my hero up and down. How are you ready to react to your hero's love and contributions in your life at his old age?

The love of parents to their sons and daughters cannot be equaled but you can do your best in returning a fair percentage of their love to you. It is possible to have another wife or husband, but you have only one biological parents in life. Honour and care for them in love.

WAYS TO CARE FOR YOUR PARENTS:

There are so many ways you can care for your parents. However, I recommend that you start from the basic necessities they provided for you at the beginning.

SHELTER: As you settle down in life, there is need to turn your searchlight towards the place where your parents live. Find out if they have a comfortable accommodation. Are they still in the same room where they lived while paying your fees and bills?

Are they protected from rain, sunshine, exposure and cold?

While you plan to live in your mansions in town, do your best to help them get an affordable housing, to ensure that they are properly sheltered.

FOOD: Always keep in touch with your parents and ask after their welfare. Food is as important as it was then. Be sure that they have food in their store house. Don't allow them to engage in compulsory fasting as a result of lack of food.

A young man collapsed in the church one day, Ushers and prayer warriors were drafted to revive him. After sometime of prayer someone suggested we look for a bottle of soft drink, who knows, per adventure, if he has not eaten. There the answer was hidden. The moment he took a bottle of soft drink, he stood and started worshipping God. Think about that.

God's long-life plan consist of determination to love the lord, our God with all our heart, wise eating habits, respect for those in authority and moderation in all things in life. Can you see where your help is needed to prolong the life of your parents? They need your honour and care, to eat wisely because it takes availability of options to make choices.

A parent that has one type of meal to eat from Sunday to Saturday cannot eat wisely. How can a hungry parent develop good eating habits when he has no list to choose from?

CLOTHING: It is a laughable adage in Igbo land, if a king has no garments. They ask, is it all kings that have clothes? Should your father be added to that list? What of your mother? They bought you your first clothes, shoes, sunshade, wristwatch and other useful wears. Please get in touch with your parents and confirm if they have good wears.

It is common knowledge these days in many places,to see a young man spend more on his new girlfriend or acquaintance within few months than he has on his parents in 15 years.

Carelessness over your parents or complete refusal

to care for your parents is an invitation to sudden poverty.

ACCESS TO DRINKING WATER: Many Parents are still faced with the challenge of trekking or cycling kilometers to fetch water to use on daily basis. Since the public water division or corporation exists mainly on paper these days, you should endeavor to provide parents with borehole. This will save them the stress of going long distance to fetch water. Water is a basic necessity and not luxury.

MEDICAL CHECKUP: Arrange for a nearby Clinic where your parents should be encouraged to visit for medicals. Young people are living on supplements already, while the parents have no access to multivitamins and antibiotics. What a wonderful world.

As you buy your supplement remember to fetch the pain reliefs and blood tonics for your parents. They should be encouraged to live long and save you the cost of organizing Africa's Largest Party- funeral service, May God give the understanding we need here in Jesus Name.

TRANSPORT FACILITY: Provide affordable and economical car or bus for your parents to get to important places like church, market and roadside farms that are away from home. On the other hand, you can arrange standby pick up cabs for them as at when necessary.

There are serviceable and affordable cars that are useful back home. Get them where you are and send them home for the comfort of your parents. Old age is so unique that David had to shout at a time in his life.

"Cast me not off in the time of old age; forsake me not when my strength faileth".

Psalm 71:9

EMPOWERMENT: Help your parents undergo short term empowerment courses if they are still strong and willing to keep themselves busy and assist them with startup capital to set up mini shops or business centres.

Honourariun: Decide on a monthly, bi-monthly or quarterly amount of cash to be given to your parents. They need it. They may not ask you. Make it a habit for them to receive bank alerts from you.

INVEST THROUGH THEM: Through the advice and information of your parents, you can acquire properties back home at affordable prices. In Future you will be grateful to them for their wise counsel and deputation.

HOLIDAY TRIPS: Whenever it is affordable by you think of surprising your parents with holiday trips to towns or any country of your choice. However, if your parents are the type that don't like travelling to other towns and nations, then you are discharged on this subject matter.

MORAL SUPPORT: Money is not everything. Money is what money can buy. Money is a defence. Old age could be very challenging if not properly planned for. Sometimes it could be very frustrating. The same way we came, we often return home.

At old age parents need the same care that you were given as a baby. That's why old peoples' home exists. But here in Africa we don't have too many of them. Parents suffer loneliness and lack of care.

Sometimes, they have money under their pillow but they may not have someone to help buy what they need with it.

Visiting your parents from time to time boost their moral aspect of living, Imagine the joy of seeing you visiting with your children.But many parents have grandchildren they have not seen for a longtime. You are also robbing your children of the opportunity of being blessed by their grandparents.

Consider the case of Joseph and his sons, Ephraim and Manasseh. They shared Jacob's full blessings because they were physically present as his hands were laid on them before pronouncing the blessings.

Money is what money can buy. Money is not everything. Go beyond money and give your parents moral support today. Even if you have arranged for a nurse to look after your old parents, do your best to show physical presence from time to time. They need you.

CELEBRATE YOUR PARENTS: Please if your parents are privileged to be alive as I write, you must stop what you are doing long enough to celebrate them. They are heroes and heroines.

POINT TO YOUR PARENTS' TOMBS: Many years after, the tomb where Jesus Christ was buried is visibly there and many visit the site till date. Are your parents dead? If you answered positive.
Are you sure you can point to your parents tombs? An affordable marble plaque is enough to remind and point people to your parent's tomb. Think over it. They were there for you.

REWARDS FOR HONOUR AND CARE FOR PARENTS:

There are so many benefits or reward that accrues to everyone that honours and cares for parents. Here are some but not all.

DOORS OF BLESSINGS OPEN TO YOU: Since the command to honour and care for your parents is of God, you qualify for God's blessing on those who obey His word because to honour parents is to Honour and obey the Lord thy God.

"AND IT shall come to pass, if thou shall hearken diligently unto the voice of the LORD thy God, to observe and to do all his commandments which I command thee this day, that the LORD thy God will set thee on high above all nations of the earth".
Deuteronomy 28:1

Each time you honour your father and mother you open yourself to blessings from God.

YOU QUALIFY FOR LONG LIFE ON EARTH: God's promise of long life is so clearly spelt out in the scripture as reward to those who honour their parents. I strongly believe that access to good medical facilities is not the primary reason for longevity, it has so much to do with obedience to God's word in Exodus 20:12. If you desire to live long here on earth, honour and care for your parents.

"Honour thy father and thy mother: that thy days may be long upon the land which the lord thy God giveth thee".
Exodus 20:12

PARENTAL BLESSINGS: A careful study of the scriptures has shown that those who took time to honour and care for their parents received parental blessings for their actions. Those who dishonoured their parents lost their positions.

Abel got blessed, Cain lost out. Isaac got blessed, Ishmael lost out. Jacob got blessed, Esau lost out. Ruth got blessed, Oprah lost out. Esther got blessed, Vashti lost out. Judah got blessed, Reuben lost out. Esau had grieved his parents already by marrying Hittite ladies before the issue of the birthright.

34. And Esau was forty years old when he took to wife Judith the daughter of Beeri, the Hittite and Bashemath the daughter of Elon the Hittite.
35. Which were a grieve of mind unto Isaac and to Rebekah.

Genesis 26:34-35

That was dishonourable and grievous to his parents. Isaac glued to his father Abraham in honour and care till death. If Jacob's [Israel] love for Joseph was not reciprocated with honour and care for Jacob [Israel], I bet you, his father wouldn't have retained his old age love for Joseph.

Ruth's refusal to disconnect from Naomi but kept faith in honour and care through service paid off. For Queen Esther her greatest concern was how to obey, honour and care for her step-parents and instead the lord favoured her.

FAVOUR BEFORE GOD AND HUMANS: Sons and daughters who honour and care for their parents, enjoy the favour of God and human beings. Their spiritual and social status grow rapidly.

And Jesus increased in wisdom and stature, and in favour with God and man.

Luke 2:52

Do you want to enjoy supernatural and natural favour? If you answered positive, then honour and care for your parents.

INHERITANCE: Every parent strives to leave an inheritance for his children, but they go extra mile to bestow something worthy on those that honoured, and cared for them.

Abraham gave gift to Ishmael while he bestowed his estate on Isaac. Whereas some sons of Jacob [Israel] struggled to get blessed Joseph got double portion. Stay close, honourable and caring to your parents.

REIGN ON THE THRONE: Sons and daughters who take steps to honour and care for their parents stand good chances of reigning on the throne of their parents. The issue of birthright is no longer based on age. Anybody can come from the backseat to the throne. Ask Esau, Reuben and Adonijah. Be wise.

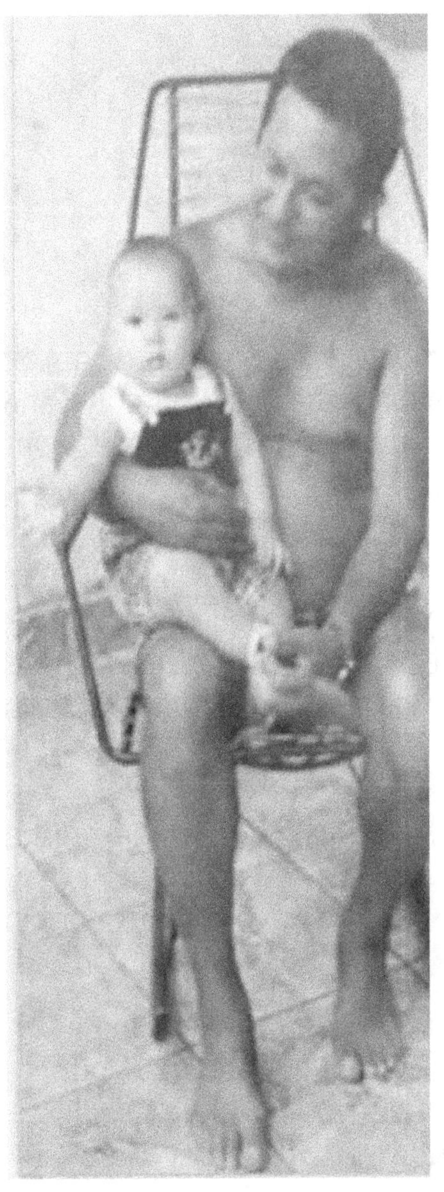

**Your father was
not left out in your
nursery stage**

3
MAJOR WAYS WE DISHONOUR OUR PARENTS:

Here are some of the ways we dishonour our parents. Look at the list humbly and crosscheck your actions towards your parents.

DISOBEDIENCE TO PARENTS: I strongly believe that disobedience to parents on Godly instructions is very dishonourable. If the advice or instructions of your parents are Godly, it is dishonourable to disobey them.

CHILDREN OBEY your parents in the lord: for this is right.

Ephesians 6:1

SPEAKING EVIL OF PARENTS: It is dishonourable to engage in speaking evil of your parents. God sees that as a major dishonour to your parents. Please, reconsider your position on this issue.

If Apostle James cautioned against speaking of evil of your brother, how much more of your parents.

[See James 4:11].

TALKING BACK AT YOUR PARENTS: Most people think it is boldness to talk back at their parents but there is no wisdom in that.

Thy tongue deviseth mischiefs: like a sharp razor, working deceitfully.

Psalm 52:2

KEEPING MALICE AND ANGER AGAINST YOUR PARENTS: Living with anger against your parents is deadly. Keep away from malice and anger from your father and mother that it may be well with you.

If you think they have offended or abandoned you at a time of help in your life, go to them in humility and sort out things with them.

But now ye also put off all these: anger, wrath, malice, blasphemy, filthy communication out of your mouth.

Colossians 3:8

HITTING YOUR PARENT PHYSICALLY: It is dishonourable to attempt fighting or hitting your parent. Most people are guilty of this gross dishonour to God. Please repent today, and if you know anybody who is guilty of this offence, reach out to him or her. why beat your father or mother? God guarantees your destruction if you continue in this dishonour.

"And he that smiteth his father, or his mother, shall be surely put to death".

Exodus 21:15

WALKING OUT ON YOUR PARENTS: It is very dishonorable and degrading to walk out on your parents while they are admonishing you no matter how hot or offensive their words may be. Keep your cool and win through apology and humility.

KEEPING MUTE, IGNORING AND OVER REACTING WHEN YOUR PARENTS ASK QUESTIONS: Doing any of the above is an act of dishonour to your parents. Arguing over instructions and similar things are not honorable.

"Hearken unto thy father that begat thee, and despise not thy mother when she is old".

Proverbs 23:22.

LYING TO PARENTS: It is dishonourable to lie to your father and your mother. Lying causes affliction to people and ruin to your parent who believe in you. *A lying tongue hateth those that are afflicted by it; and a flattering mouth worketh ruin.*

Proverb 26:28.

STURBBORNESS AND REBELLION: Sons and daughters who are stubborn and rebellious to parents attract God's anger and judgment. Stubbornness and rebellion to parents leads to death. You can confirm from Absalom.

18. If a man has a stubborn and rebellious son, which will not obey the voice of his father, or the voice of his mother, and that, when they have chastened him will not hearken to them:

19. Then shall his father and his mother lay hold on him, and bring him out unto the elders of his city, and unto the gate of his place:

20.And they shall say unto the elders of his city, this our son is stubborn and rebellious he would not obey our voice: he is a. glutton and a drunkard.

21.And all the men of his city shall stone him with stones that he die: so shall thou put evil away from among you: and all Israel shall hear and fear.

Deuteronomy 21:18-21

A rebellious son or daughter is a constant source of grief to his or her parents. Think!

SHOUTING AT YOUR PARENTS: Today, young boys and girls derive pleasure from cussing, huffing and yelling at their parents at their own peril. If you are guilty of this misbehavior get out of it urgently, let it be done now.   **[See psalms 52:2].**

MOCKING YOUR PARENTS: I have seen foolish sons and daughters who clap and mock their parents in public and go home and expect their own children to honour them.

Sorry, you can't plant banana and harvest plantain, though they are close in resemblance. The foolish children that mocked Elisha did not go home to share their experiences.

[See 2Kings 2:23-24].

SNEAKING STRANGERS TO THE HOUSE [BOYS/GIRLS]: These days we see young ones resist the power of their parents. They smuggle in boys and girls into the house without the knowledge of their parents to indulge in irresponsible conducts, until they are exposed. This is very dishonourable. Please desist from it.

[See Romans 13:2].

PUTTING UP SHAMEFUL ACTIONS OUTSIDE THE HOUSE: There are sons and daughters who have dual faces - one in the house, another outside the house. They are so wonderful, calm and holy at home but the opposite of godliness outside the home. Some of them live like saints in the house and live like Satan outside the house.

As I watch school boys and girls smoke and stock their school bags with sachets of dry gin and cigarettes, I wonder if they are the same virgins and eunuchs at home. What a generation? When I watch girls and boys move from Saturday night clubs to choir seats on Sunday mornings? I ask God for mercy.

The question is: Who is fooling who? Is it the young people who allow themselves to be destroyed thinking that they are cheating their parents or the men and women who lure these young ones into the satanic traps thinking that their own children are safe and saints at home?

SIGHING AND ROLLING EYES ON PARENTS: We have a generation of young people who sigh and roll their eyes at their parents as they are rebuked. They puff and huff in foolishness and arrogance. May God deliver this generation of internet learners.

INGRATITUDE: Unthankfulness is sinful and a mark of ingratitude. It is not only dishonourable to deny your parents gratitude, it is equally shameful and a proof of complete disobedience to God.

"THIS KNOW also, that in the last days' perilous times shall come. For men shall be lovers of their own selves, covetous, boasters, proud, blasphemers disobedient to parents, unthankful, unholy".

II Timothy 3:1-2

REFUSAL TO LISTEN TO PARENTS: We have this extreme group of people who don't listen to their parents, they don't sit down with them, they don't believe they should be there. If you give them the opportunity they can use their parents for money rituals. They refuse to listen to their parents and go all out to despise them in so many ways. Please beware of such sons and daughters.

[See 2 Timothy 3:1-4].

WORSHIP OF PARENTS MORE THAN GOD: It is also noteworthy that only God should be God in our lives. Any parent that exalts himself or herself above God should be reminded that it is unscriptural to love any parent more than God.

That is why I began this chapter with the statement that all instructions must be godly and not ungodly. So any parent that discourages you from worshipping the God of Abraham, Isaac and Jacob must be brought to order in humility and scriptural wisdom. Loving your parents more than God is not honourable but idol worship.

However, let no son or daughter capitalize on the above caution to dishonour his or her parents because l believe that every wise parent will always teach his or her children to love and worship the almighty God.

"He that loveth father or mother more than me is not worthy of me:and he that loveth son or daughter more than me is not worthy of me".

Matthew10:37

REFUSAL OF CARE: It is dishonourable to have and fail to care for your mother and father. It is unacceptable, it is wickedness, and it is disobedience to God and man. It is quick loss of memory of how God helped you through them.

SUEING PARENTS TO COURT: It is not advisable to take your parents to court. Do your best to seek amicable settlement with them irrespective of the magnitude of disagreement or offence. It is wrongful and shameful to take your parents to law courts and watch another person's parent rule over you and your own parents.

God is even unhappy with believers who engage in lawsuits. If God detests watching you and your fellow believer in Christ go to court for civil matters, how would he feel over your resolve to take your parents to court.
Wouldn't it be better that you suffer loss or bear the pain for parents who have suffered and endured every pain for you in life? [See 1Corinthians 6:1-7]

HAVING A BABY BEFORE MARRIAGE: It is dishonourable to have a child while unmarried in your parent's house. Whether you are a boy or girl you must overcome the lust of the flesh by running away from the dishonour of raising children while unmarried and living with your parents.

CURSING YOUR PARENTS: it is very dangerous to curse your parents. Offenders are liable to die young. The word of God guarantees that.

Whosoever curseth his father or mother his lamp shall be put out in obscure darkness.
Proverbs 20:20

VISIBLE SIGNS OF FOOLISHNESS:

Sons and daughters who take pleasure in dishonouring their parents only demonstrate how foolish they are to the public. Show me a man or woman who dishonours parents and I will show you a fool.

"A wise son maketh a glad father: but a foolish man despiseth his mother. Folly is joy to him that is destitute of wisdom, but a man of understanding walketh uprightly".
Proverbs 15:20-21

**Your Hero leading in struggles,
love and care**

4
DANGERS OF DISHONOURING YOUR PARENTS

DISOBEDIENCE TO GOD: When you choose to dishonour your parents, you have chosen to disobey God who commanded you to honour your parents. [See Exodus 20:12].

UNTIMELY DEATH: When you dishonour your parents you lose the benefit of long life on earth. Sons and daughters who toe the line of dishonour to their parents take early exit from planet Earth.

Don't waste your time arguing on this truth. Simply do your best to honour and care for your parents.

"Honour thy father and mother: which is the first commandment with promise: That it may be well with thee and thou mayest live long on the earth".
Ephesians 6:2,3

YOU SUFFER SHAME AND DISHONOUR: If you choose to dishonour your parents, you must be ready to face shame and dishonour at the fullness of time.

The bible says that none was found to be as fair as Absalom in the land of Israel. That probably made him forget that he came out of David.

I.   He engaged his father in physical battles.
ii.   Chased him away from the royal palace.
iii. Slept with ten of his concubines in the open.
iv.   Determined to kill his father and take over the throne forcefully.

What happened? Absalom died shamefully, painfully, dishonourably, untimely, rejected by the heavens and the earth at death. He was hanged on an oak tree, taken up between the heavens and earth. [See 2Samuel 18:1-17].

YOU LOSE YOUR BIRTHRIGHT: Sons and daughters who dishonour their parents risk losing their birthright or outright disowning by their parents.

The man Reuben was the first son of Jacob but his dishonour of sleeping with his father's concubine on his father's bed robbed him of his birthright and excellence in life.   [See Genesis 49:3-4].

What of Esau who chose a lifestyle in the opposite direction of his parents. He kept acquiring Hittite ladies as wives when he knew that it was a source of grief to his parents.

Esau had lost the favour of his parents already before the formal bestowal of the birthright on Jacob by Isaac. Can you catch the revelation?

A LIFE OF SUFFERING: Dishonouring your parents may lead to a lifetime of suffering. Many who rough handled their parents and ran to towns and cities ended up living in hardship and penury until they died or encountered Jesus Christ, made U-turn and apologized to their parents.

Prosperity is not for sons and daughters who dishonour their parents. [See Ephesians6:3].

LOSS OF RELATIONSHIP: Dishonouring your father or mother may sever your relationship with them as parents. Remember, they represent God to a large extent, living in enmity with your parents is dangerous.

"For the son dishonoureth the father, the daughter riseth against her mother, the daughter-in-law against her mother-in-law: a man's enemies are the men of his own house".   **Micah 7:6**

CURSES: Parents who continually face dishonour and lack of care from their children, turn to curse them at heart. This hidden, unpronounced but clearly spelt evil expectation or imagination against you is very dangerous. Some delayed breakthroughs and blessings of the womb are products of parental curses.

Parents, are hereby, cautioned to desist from such pronounced and unpronounced curses. (See Deuteronomy 27:16)

YOU LOSE THEIR INTERCESSORY ROLE: Parents are great intercessors for their children. Their prayers prevent tragedies from occurring in the lives of their children. Many years after Lot separated from Abraham, he [Lot] was still enjoying the prayer covering of Abraham.

It was the prayer of Abraham that saved Lot and his two daughters from destruction when God's judgment was delivered on Sodom and Gomorrah.

A MARK OF STURBORNESS, REBELLION, GLUTTONY AND DRUNKENESS: Refusal to honour and care for your parents is a proof of stubbornness and rebellion against them. This may lead to their recommendation of stoning you to the elders.

When your parents' hand you over to the elders of the city for stoning, you face the danger of sudden death by evil forces.

And they shall say unto the elders of his city, this our son is stubborn and rebellious he would not obey our voice: he is a. glutton and a drunkard.

Deuteronomy 21:20

WHY PEOPLE CONSIDER DISHONOUR:

There is no action without reason. Here are some reasons why some sons and daughters attempt or consider the part of dishonour to parents instead of honour.

GETTING INTO TROUBLE FOR A NON-BIG DEAL: One major reason why people consider dishonouring their parents is the fear of getting into a bigger trouble with their parents over an issue or action they consider minor. They think discussing the issue with their parents may blow it out of proportion, because to them it is not a big deal.

DEMANDING REASON FOR THE INSTRUCTION:
Most stubborn and disobedient children would rather want to know your reason for advising them not to take a particular course. If you fail to provide an answer or give an unsatisfactory answer, you risk their dishonour.

OLD VERSUS NEW SCHOOL MENTALITY:
Sometimes children dishonour or consider dishonouring their parents because they think that they will not understand the subject matter.

DOUBT YOU WILL LISTEN: When people doubt that you will give them attention on what is bothering them, they push for dishonourable steps to achieve their aims.

BEING EMBARRASSED PUBLICLY: When children feel that they have been embarrassed in the public by their parents, they may take dishonourable actions to get out of the situation. This is more likely if the embarrassment is before their friends.

FORESEE UNFAVOURABLE ANSWER: if children doubt that your answer to their question will be favourable to them. They may avoid asking you in the first place, if they have taken a decision already, and they doubt your advice will not favour them, then forget it. You will not be approached at all.

PROVOCATIONS/TOXICITY:

"And, ye fathers provoke not your parents to wrath but bring them up in the nurture and admonition of the Lord".

Ephesians 6:4

So much has been written in this book on sons' and daughters' dishonor of parents. As much as possible parents should do their best in addressing their part in relationship. There are so many ways parents lead their children to anger. Let us do our best to avoid provocations/self-centredness in our relationship with our children.

HOW PARENTS PROVOKE THEIR CHILDREN:
Here are some but not all the ways parents provoke their sons and daughters to anger.

OVERLOADED EXPECTATIONS:
Parents should be careful with what they expect

from their sons and daughters. Unrealistic expectation from sons and daughters by their parents may lead to provocations on the part of the children.

Sometimes, it is better to allow your son or daughter put up positive surprise than holding onto unrealizable expectations. Give them time to grow, develop, understand, think and overcome childishness.

"When I was a child, I spake as a child, I understood as a child, I thought as a child, but when I became a man, I put away childish things".
1Corinthian 13:11

REVERSAL OF UNGUARDED FREEDOM: Parents should overcome the temptation of giving too much freedom to their children. At a certain time in life freedom should be guarded by parents through the rod and reproof. Trying to reverse unguarded freedom later in life causes serious provocation. A child should not be left to his or her world to rot (See proverbs2.9:15)

BEING TOO STRICT: Much as it is not advisable to give too much freedom to the child, it is provoking to get too strict with your children.

Raise them up in fear and wisdom of God, trust, peace, gentleness, exemplary lifestyle free from hypocrisy. Overcome partiality and suspicion, trusting God to perfect all that concerns your children.

"But the wisdom that is from above is first pure then peaceable, gentle and easy to be entreated, full of mercy and good fruits, without partiality, and without hypocrisy".

James 3:17

LACK OF AFFIRMATION: Parents should be affirmative in decision making at all times. Take a firm position on issues that requires correction or assertions.

But once that is done you must reaffirm your love and faith on the child to avoid losing the child to the public or the devil. Once the correction is given, don't dwell there, move forward., or expect provocation for dwelling there.

RIDICULING PROVOKES: Whatever happens, avoid ridiculing or mocking your child. Trust God to change and turn him her over to you. Don't let anyone think his or her world is finished. Be an encourager not a mocker.

ABUSIVE STATEMENT: Parents are advised to avoid the use of abusive words on their children. It is true that some of their actions are very provocative, but patience can overcome a lot of provocations.

CONTINUOUS FAULT FINDING: Some parents are guilty of constant fault finding about their children. This can be very provoking and discouraging to the overall development of the child.

Let's not play God in their lives, but provide an enabling environment for them to joyfully and Godly develop.

CALLING OF NICKNAMES: Often we are pushed to the wall of calling nicknames and bad names to retaliate the wrong actions of our children. Please, do your best to overcome that temptation

ANGRY REACTIONS: Rebuking children in our anger could be dangerous and destructive. Please, ask God to help you overcome that challenge by keeping a quiet spirit during such moments.
When you react later you save life and avoid injuries on the other party. The psalmist knew the danger of angry reactions. Hear what he says:

"O LORD, rebuke me not in thine anger, neither chasten me in thy hot displeasure".

Psalm 6:1

A NO WRONG POSITION: That you are a parent does not mean that you can't be wrong in your actions. A situation whereby parents maintain a no wrong position is unscriptural and provocative.

If you get it wrong, accept your mistake, apologize and move forward. That does not rub you of your royal position as father or mother.

INCONSISTENT DISCIPLINE: Maintain a constant position on discipline. Taking action against one and leaving others when they offend is inconsistent. Don't delay corrections.

"Because sentence against an evil work is not executed speedily, therefore the heart of the sons of men is fully set in them to do evil".

Ecclesiastes 8:11

COMPARISMS: Parents are tempted to compare their children with others. It is not good. It slows down the moral of the child and leads to inferiority complex. God created us in-compare, that is why everyone of us is uniquely made.

Comparing your child with another is not only provoking to the child, God is not pleased with that action, because it looks as if He has created a deficiency in your child.

BROKEN PROMISES: Parents should overcome the short coming of promise and fail. When you make promises to your children, do fulfill them or renew them with genuine explanations.

YELLING AT CHILDREN BEFORE THEIR FRIENDS: As much as possible, parents should avoid public yelling at their children in the name of correction. Parents will achieve more in terms of results if such a child is talked to one on one.

REFUSAL TO LISTEN TO CHILDREN'S OPINIONS OR SUGGESTIONS: Parents who refuse to listen to the opinions or suggestions of their children create wrong impression of themselves to their children. Find time to listen to your children's opinions.

Their suggestions may be the key to solving the puzzle. Our sons and daughters feel unhappy and insecure when they are not given the opportunity to explain themselves

HYPOCRITICAL LIFESTYLE: Children are often provoked when they discover that their parents live the opposite of the lifestyle they recommend for them. Teaching your children to do what is different from what you do is hypocrisy.

Teaching or instructing your children through exemplary lifestyle is the best. The ideology of "do what I say and not what I do is hypocrisy.

DISHONOURABLE MARITAL LIFE: Our children will be pleased to see us overcome marital dishonour, tension, fighting, separation, suspicion and quarrelling. Those actions send wrong signals to our children about marriage.

Sometimes they are provoked to take sides which is equally wrongful. Parents should avoid provoking their children through unholy activities and behaviours.

WASTEFUL LIVING: Children are often disappointed and provoked when they discover that their parents have lived or are living a wasteful life.

Parents who borrow uncontrollably and pledge or sell off their properties or estate without consulting their children are not showing Godly and goodly example to their children

DRUNKENNESS, LAZINESS AND GLUTTONY:

Some parents refuse to stay away from drunkenness, too much food and laziness.

This provocation is rampant among male parents, who though they are healthy refuse to work to provide for the family.

Rather than do that, they go about drinking, overfeeding and sleeping while men go to work, thereby, pushing the responsibility to their wives to fend for the family. This is very discouraging to children. Our men should please work on this point.

There are also mothers who are so lazy and drunken that they cannot manage the kitchen but go to buy ready-made food outside.

DIVORCE: Children who have watched their parents live and work as one in sufferings, lows and highs in life, are provoked to anger when they see their parents part ways because of minor issues that can be easily settled in love.

Parents who divorce create opportunity for children to take sides. God hates divorce.

**Sweet mother combining all
to save cost**

5

POWER OF PARENTAL BLESSING

Ensure that you obtain the blessing of your parents while living with them, when leaving the home for personal exploits and while living independently. This you can do by maintaining a strong communication link with them wherever you are. The need for parental blessing cannot be over emphasized.

For 75 years, Abraham could not achieve much, until God chose him and did what his father forgot to do for him- God blessed Abraham. God did not give any cash to Abraham as he was leaving home. God blessed him. (See Genesis 12:1-3)

Parental Blessing is primary to your success in life. Don't make it a secondary issue. Ask young men and womenwho disconnected from their parents and ran to town how life has been unfair to them.

Parental blessing was so highly valued in the Old Testament, and the value hasn't changed till date.

The patriarchs Abraham, Isaac and Jacob all gave formal blessing to their children. In the case of Jacob, he extended the blessing to his grandchildren Ephraim and Manasseh. Isaac's blessing on Jacob which was originally meant for Esau gave him the earth's bounty and dominion of his brother Esau.

Most of the time the parental blessings included words of encouragement, details concerning one's inheritance, and prophetic declaration relating to the person's future.

In Jacob's blessing to Judah, it was so clearly stated that his brothers will praise him, his hand will be on the neck of his enemies, his father's sons will bow down before him, and that Kings will come out of him.

Judah's descendants later gave birth to King David on whose land Jerusalem is located. Jesus Christ also came from the tribe of Judah.

(See Mathew 1:3, Genesis 49:8-10)

Don't joke with parental blessing. Get closer to your parents. Closeness to your parents offers them the opportunity to cancel any illegal or offensive pronouncements they have made against you in your developmental stages in life.

PARENTS SHOULD PASS ON BLESSINGS NOT CURSES: Children are God's arrows in the hands of their parents. It is the responsibility of parents to launch their children very far in life through prophetic blessings and educational development or empowerment.

It is the responsibility of parents to shoot their children into the future, equipped in knowledge, wealth, power and wisdom that they have gained in life and those obtained from their forefathers'. However, our greatest challenge as parents is that we have continued to abort our future generations through curses, family disorder and ignorance.

I hereby, appeal to parents to do their best to pray and bless their sons and daughters and not curse them.

But our sons and daughters should be wise to run away from self-imposed curses. For instance, you cannot be in a girlfriend's house shouting babe kill me with love under the influence of tramadol while your parents are at home praying for you to have long life. You cannot be calling for death while your parents are praying for life. You may eventually die because your personal prayer and desire receives quicker answer. Life and death are in the power of the tongue.

THE LAW OF SOWING AND REAPING:

While the earth remaineth, seedtime and harvest, and cold and heat, and summer and winter, and day and night shall not cease.

Genesis 8:22

THE NEW ORDER: At the end of Noah's world, God instituted a new order of living here on earth. It is known as the order or law of sowing and reaping.

The law of sowing and reaping is not only a supernatural law, but also a natural law. Ignorance is a deadly virus that serves as lubrication oil for poverty and failure. We are told that ignorance is not an excuse in law.

Life is governed by certain laws that ignorance of them will cause you untold hardship in life. These laws should govern our actions and inactions here on earth, especially when we grow up to the age of accountability. The law of sowing and reaping was not instituted by man. Some people erroneously refer to it as the law of karma. God simply wants us to watch over our actions towards one another. Nobody likes the negative aspect of the law of sowing and reaping.

Everybody seems to desire receiving only good from the Lord. However, Job deferred on the issue, when he said that he should not expect to receive only good from the Lord. Nobody likes the negative aspect of the law of sowing and reaping.

SEEDTIME: On daily basis we sow seeds of goodness. In the same order bad seeds take roots when they are sowed through our wrong actions and decisions **(Gal 1:7).**

If they are not uprooted on time, they grow and bear fruits. The fruit of a bad seed is what some people call return match or payback period. If you have sowed a bad seed, uproot it and repent from sowing further bad seeds.

If those seeds were sown in the days of darkness, confess them to the Lord and desist from further activities of darkness. The lord will hear and your harvest will pass through the blood of Jesus Christ. The atonement for sin by the blood of Jesus will affect your harvest considerably.

The reason is that God is a righteous judge, that is why He is called our Justice. The blood of Jesus makes it difficult for any of us believers in Christ to receive the equivalent of our bad seeds. What you call punishment from God, would have been more disastrous if not for the mercies of God through the blood of Jesus Christ.

BAD ATTITUDES TOWARDS PARENTS ARE SEEDS:

We have to watch our actions and inactions towards our parents, because overtime, they will become seeds that are subject to harvest. Let the development of your own children not disconnect you from your parents. Do unto your parents what you expect your children to do to you in future. This is called the law of likeability- doing to others what you would like them to do to you.

Pause, think of your love and concerns for your

children. Your parents did not do less for you. In my thinking they did more because they went through adverse conditions to love, cherish, train and defend your wrong actions.

LOOK AT THIS EXAMPLE:

At the wake of the Nigeria - Biafra Civil war, we only ran along with only whatever, we could carry on our heads. Whatever we could not carry was left behind, and lost to thieves and hoodlums. On return my mom sold the wrappers she had left, to enable us eat.

At a time, she had only one wrapper to go to church and an old in house clothe to use at home. For her to wash the regular wrapper, she has to wake up early, draw up her dross up to cover her breast before the washing. She also had to stay indoors until the house clothes are dried up. Some parents have worse experiences to share.Some accounts are so shameful and sorrowful to share

Today, it is common knowledge that some young men and women prefer to waste their estate on girlfriends and boyfriends than look after such mothers. Many fathers had cases of physical humiliations which they endured to keep the home together because they didn't want you to be raised by a single parent.

TAKE ACTION NOW:

I used my first month salary to buy a Raleigh bicycle for my mom. When things changed for us, she had a house to live in, fully furnished and secured.

People come to fetch water from her house, hang around her gates because of light, and to eat free food because it was freely available. She took in many to live with her, farm as many places as they can for free.

Back in 1992 when she slept in the Lord, she had her own car, a driver and many debtors. God restored everything she lost and added more to her. I remember being begged by a family the day I went to redeem some of our family lands held on pledge, to leave some plots of land for them.

For every Naira Mama needed to pay our school fees those days, they would ask her to release a plot of land. You would say that they tried in receiving the land on pledge, but the circumstances surrounding their help, if you so wish to call it, was very fraudulent.

My Dad was a tax collector for our divisional headquarters. That gave him the privilege of holding onto cash until the government call for quarterly returns. Many people came to beg him for assistance to start trading with whatever he could give to them, so they can use and return before the usual quarterly account.

They will collect the money but never kept to their part of the agreement, to return the loan which was interest free. When the government come asking for the money, the same people that borrowed from my father will go through the back door using somebody to suggest receiving land on pledge. Dad will say okay, instead of facing the wrath of the government or going to jail, let them take the land, one day my children will take it back. The situation worsened when Dad died.

But that was not the end of our story. God overturned everything in our favour. I prophesy to you reading this book now, God will do greater miracles of restoration in your life and estate in Jesus name. **[See Psalm 126:1-3].**

Many unprintable things were done to stop us but God was there for us. When God turned again our captivity, we did not only redeem those lands, we bought more lands. God will visit you positively to overtake and rule in Jesus Name.

THINK: Now, if you have parents that went through similar or worse experiences in life to raise you, do you need a mentor to tell you to care for them?

Back in 1992, when mama slept in the lord, the highest rated Christian band at that time was Voice of the Cross. They were invited on their own terms to play for two days during the funeral services. We did that because she had a taste of good living, before she died. A situation whereby, Millions of Naira are spent on funeral services of parents who could not be cared for while they were alive is not allowed, neither is it acceptable to the living or the dead. Let us change today in Jesus name.

Every family shine brightest in the community, when it aligns with her sons and daughters to fight the forces of darkness against their family. Your parents believe strongly in the scripture below because of you.

"For I reckon that the sufferings of this present time are not worthy to be compared with the glory which shall be revealed in us".

Roman 8:18.

They endured the pain and went through the ridicule. Today God has answered their prayers by blessing you. What are you waiting for?

THE TIME IS NOW: Lift up your head and see the redemption of your family through you. God's word is correct whether it is socially, politically correct or not. You are added to that family to lift up the name of the family from obscurity to fame.

Arise and shine as you honour and care for your parents (See Isaiah 60:1). There is a reason for that glory God has released upon you. Let it radiate on your family of orientation as it is radiating on our family of procreation.

As parents, they gave their hearts to you. You must unite in their vision, pursuit of generational blessings and continuity of the throne. As a child, you were a loan that God gave to them and they were able to shoot you very far like an arrow into a glorious future. You are their heritage from the Lord.

BE PROUD OF YOUR PARENTS: At every point in life, you should be proud to say that's my Daddy or that's my mummy. One major reason why you are being blessed is so you can be a blessing to your parents as well as your immediate family.

Don't forget that our God is the God of generations: The God of Abraham, Isaac and Jacob. Some of the visions given to your parents may be accomplished by you. Likewise, some of the visions that will be given to you by God may be accomplished by your children. The reason is that no true vision is accomplished in one life time only. If you are in the Spirit, catch the fire now.

As you respond to the abandoned visions of your family, other brothers and sisters will rise up and join forces with you. This is the time, season and day to act. Start now

KEEP THE LIGHT BURNING: Keep the light of your family burning. Don't allow it to be sniffed off in Jesus Name. It is your responsibility to move your generation to a new and greater glory by empowering every hand to work. Your family should be that family on a hill that radiates light.

DON'T EXPOSE YOUR PARENTS TO SHAME: Please, don't expose your parents to shame. Many parents surrendered their goodwill to feed their families. I can still recall memories of some people whose parents were stripped and paraded round the communities immediately after the war because they harvested Cassava from another person's farm, to feed their Children. Their lives were cut short because of the shame. As I write this book, their children find it difficult to associate with others because of the memory of that episode.

Till date, there are women who sleep with other men to keep food on their Children's table. Likewise, there are men who sleep with sugar mummies against their will to ensure that family bills are paid. It takes a high level of courage and grace of God to walk away from a man or woman who has submitted your particulars to the bank as signatory to his or her bank account. I can boldly tell you that it takes grace to walk away from wealth that has been created already.

A counselee once confided in me that her mother-in-law told her that adultery is not bad, because its proceeds are used in training the children. Can such a woman look unto her husband for provision? The man knew already how his mother managed to develop him and he expects the wife to follow suit.

A responsible parent must have suffered one form

of affliction or the other in training and development of a child. Please, honour and care for your parents. Whether your parents have been as helpful, caring, loving, encouraging, supportive as you expected or not do your best to show gratitude to them, without them you would not have been in this part of the world.

Nothing could be more urgent than thank you. Let them know that you appreciate their roles and contributions to your birth, upbringing, and development.

**A disappointed father.
Is your father happy?**

6

OLD AGE & RELATIONSHIP CHALLENGES

As infants, we glued to our mother's breasts. As teenagers we glued to the kitchen food cabinet. As adolescents we run away from home because of errands. As youths we seek independence and separation through marriage and work. The wise sons and daughters visit regularly and extend care.

However, as time flies. We see something strange in the relationship that exists between these same people and their parents. We see cases of hatred and abandonment of parents. We see sons and daughters who disown their parents, and parents who disown their children.

Some children prevent their parents from accessing their homes and family members. We see parents who go to law court with their children over minor disputes.

We see cases of wickedness against each other to the extent that some people use their parents for money rituals and vice versa. We encounter cases of people who sever relationship and communication with parents and family members.

What about fighting and quarreling with parents. We see cases of parents telling their sons and daughters to move out of their compound and related issues like that. We see parents, sons and daughters curse each other for earthly things. We see parents who love and hate some of their children. We encounter cases of gang up against father or against mother by children teaming up with their mother or father.

We see hatred and favouritism in the transfer of birthright and inheritance. We see blessings on some sons and daughters and curses on others. All that ought not to be so.

Parents and their children should do their best to overcome the provocation at this stage in family relationship, because this is the stage at which transfer of generational blessing is lost or gained. This is the point at which blessing or curses are transferred to the next generation.

Sons and daughters should be wise enough to win this satanic upset against their relationship with parents, for that is a major way of having better generation ahead.

How would you feel if your children rise up to fight you in future? Experiences have shown that God's anger has been on the sons and daughters of rebellion as against the parents who are supposed to be adjudged wrong. The reason is that God cannot contradict His word:

"Honour thy father and thy mother that thy days may be long upon the land which the lord thy God giveth thee".

What of sons and daughters who rise up to dethrone their parents and enthrone themselves?
What of those who adopt strangers as Parents?
We see people who gang up and plot rebellion against father or mother.

We see sons who force their mothers out of their matrimonial homes. We see sons and daughters who leave home and refuse to visit their parents for five, ten, twenty, thirty years and above.

Some read the obituary announcement of their parents on newspapers.
We see sons and daughters who try to give the wrong impression that marriage is bad by blaming their spouse for their carelessness and wickedness against their parents.

Think of it, these are sons and daughters raised to take over and take charge. What a WORLD!

GIVE BEFITTING LIVING BEFORE BEFITTING BURIAL: There is an evil which I have seen under the sun, and it is common among parents. Men and Women God has given riches, wealth and honour by way of children so that they could live happy and healthy to enjoy the goodness and reward of heritage from God, but a stranger takes over and enjoys the reward of their labour, this is truly vanity and it is an evil disease.

If your parents are blessed with one hundred children and are privileged to live many years and their souls are not filled with goodness and things that make living attractive, and also if they have no burial, one that had an untimely birth is better than them   **(See Ecclesiastes 6:1 – 2)**

A BEFITTING LIVING: I have paused a few times to think of the lives of parents, their efforts and hope for living as they work tirelessly to provide family basic necessities, education and other empowerment for their children to enable them face the future with boldness and confidence.

Parents go through all kinds of challenges to see their children through schools. Some sell their properties while others do abnormal jobs to ensure that the dream of developing their children is realized. Many parents suffer hunger, abuse, injustice, nakedness, mockery hardship, disgrace and what have you to raise their children.Some parents disobey God and take to sin to place food on the table.

Many are defrauded by people pretending to be helpers and sympathizers. Many parents die as a result of stress, lack of care and excessive labour. I know of parents that maintain three (3) different jobs so as to make ends meet. Many parents lose their lives in the course of searching for means of livelihood. I have seen mothers back children as they cook, fetch water and carry blocks at construction sites.

Those of us who believe in mental development, which some call western education start paying education bills from kindergarten homes to universities. I strongly recommend education to everyone, not just to some, because mental poverty is the worst poverty ever, and that accounts for the reason why some countries like ours are backwards. No matter how much is bequeathed to an underdeveloped person, he/she cannot live in dominion overtime, because a life of dominion is a process. It takes knowledge - Power - Resource - Authority - Influence - Dominion. It takes five progressive steps to arrive at dominion. You cannot jump to the sixth level which is a life of dominion.

That is why believers in Christ are finding it difficult to achieve a life for dominion. We just assume that prayer and fasting can take the place of other steps to dominion. Sorry, if I have offended you, but that's the truth, and there is no plus or minus to the truth. Prayer cannot replace labour.

Back to base, if your parents have gone through the challenges of raising you and they are alive as you read this book, God expects you to rise up and give your parents a befitting living. God spoke about a befitting living before a befitting burial.

No matter how long your parents live, if they cannot enjoy their prosperity, which you represent, they are suffering from an evil disease orchestrated by your lack of care.

Now is the best time, the best time to build them the house you will rush to build while their remains are deposited in the mortuary. This is the best time to paint in and out of the building so your parents can have a taste of good living. This is the best time to fence the compound and secure your parents from danger.

Why sink a borehole at death to impress visitors who were not there when your parents were suffering? Why sell your parents properties to bury them? Land does not multiply and the one your parents thought wise to leave for you as an inheritance, you are quick to transfer its ownership to another. In the name of sourcing out funds for befitting burial you want to mortgage your inheritance.

This is the best time to start giving your parents a good living. Begin where you are with what you have. No act of kindness or care is too small. Start today. Start now

A BEFITTING BURIAL
The second thing the teacher, identified as an evil disease in Ecclesiastes six is the absence of befitting burial to a worthy parent.

For a parent to have a befitting burial two basic things are necessary: A son/daughter or a trustworthy caretaker. It is not enough for a man to be wealthy, if he has no son, daughter or caretaker of his estate he/she will not get a befitting burial.
The second thing is money. A look at the two points shows that one has to do with the deceased while the other has to do with the living. It is not the public that will determine how your parents will leave the world. The issue of clothing, gasket and final resting

place is not a public thing.

It takes a son daughter or caretaker like Eleazer in Abraham's house to take such quality decisions
(see Genesis 24:2)

What we see from the above statement is that money as much as it is very necessary for a parent's burial, it does not take primary place in the burial of a noble man or woman. Having a son or daughter to direct the affairs of a mother or father's burial in the absence of any of the couple is more important than money.

People that are not qualified to access your parent's corpse may do so if there is no son or daughter to take charge. For instance, a man who planted six inches nail on my mom's path because she did not give him a place to dig latrine or toilet came to spy her, while she was lying in state. I stopped the man and reminded him that mama told me that he planted six inches nails that hurt her some time ago. I asked him before everybody why he wanted to see the remains of a person he had wanted dead many years ago? He confirmed that he did plant those nails and mama stepped on one of them. He went further to tell the public that mama survived the poisonous nails and that he accompanied her to the church for thanksgiving. He said that her death was not as a result of that nail. A wonderful world you will say.

I asked him to excuse us and he did. What if my mom had no son or daughter to oversee things? Your presence and participation in your parent's burial are more important and primary to the secondary issue of money.

YES, MONEY IS A DEFENCE: If you have cared for your parents while they were alive you are permitted to give them a befitting burial. Spending to offer to the public what you never offered to your parents while they were alive is not permitted. Spending to show off and impress your friends and colleagues at workplace is not reasonable.

Borrowing to entertain the masses in the name of honour for parents is unwise. Selling off your father's land (now your inheritance) is not a good idea. Why borrow to buy drinks, expensive clothes and cows for the living whereas your parents were not given the foretaste of your show off? Your parents never had radio to listen to news and music while alive. At death you are spending Millions to hire Musicians and dancers for people who never knew what music and dance looked like.

You think that you are entertaining people, whereas they are singing and laughing at your wasteful spending. Sometimes our wasteful spending causes problem among brethren. When we buried mama in 1992, one out of the cows we bought which was given to her people took them to the local court. The tussle was over who was the rightful owner of the cow as to get the larger share. Our challenge was that mama was the only surviving child of her parents. Nobody ever identified with us as an uncle during our rough days. At her death we decided to give the honour to the nearest elder in her place of birth.

Please, don't waste your resources in the name of befitting burial. Beware of people who create bills for you during burial ceremony of beloved one. You lose beloved father or mother, and relations are drawing long list of bills they expect you to honour. Are they charging you for the person's death?

The church has not made the challenge simple either. You lose a dear one and the church comes up with a long list of dues or levies and other requirements to meet before the person is buried. Are they trying to make the deceased debt-free in heaven or hell?

You lose a church member you are not too sure of where he or she is heading to, instead of being sober, you are busy making frivolous demands on the bereaved family. Let charity prevail in Jesus Name.

However, if you have honoured and cared for your parents unto death, joyfully give them a befitting burial at death. A befitting burial should not be a show off. It should be your last honour, care for them in remembrance of all they mean to you.

Even Ishmael whose portion in Abraham was only a gift, teamed up with Isaac who inherited Abraham's estate as their father was buried.**(See Genesis 25:9).** You are inexcusable.

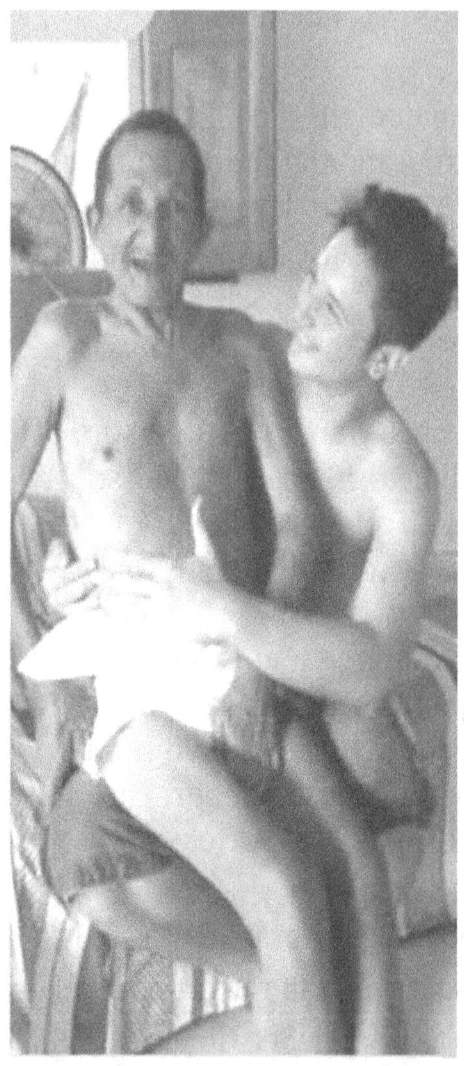

**Your father needs
care at old age**

7

AVOID GET RICH QUICK SCHEMES

*I*n your quest to make money and take care of yourself and others, there is need to throw caution to ensure that you do not run into get rich quick schemes or projects. The key to success in life is proper preparation. Whosoever decides to make quick money has desired long lasting poverty in life.

Money requires long term plans and actions of genuine labour to make or earn. House builders who use fake materials end up in regrets as the project suffers setback by way of complete demolition or partial reconstruction of faulty areas.

It is because we do not spend enough time to think before taking decisions and actions that make us fall to cheap suggestions of fraudsters. A fraudster tells you to bring the money you have to be doubled, and you are quick to go to the bank to withdraw your savings to give without reasoning, thinking or asking personal questions.

The bible is clear on the truth that those who desire quick money or riches will not go unpunished. You don't place your finger on fire without being burnt.

You tell me some people are lucky to get out of quick money schemes unhurt after they have made their money. Truth is that they still pay adequate dues. If the people who were into 419 (advanced fee fraud/other crimes) before they branched into ministry, will be humble enough to share their experiences, young people will not be in the mad rush they are today to make quick money.

Treasures of wickedness profit nothing. Whatever you obtain fraudulently leaves you with time. Don't waste your God given time to argue on the above issue. Ask God to open your eyes to a clear means of livelihood and discover that there are various ways of making genuine money here on earth.

Ask God to show you the way or simply subject yourself to genuine professionals/teachers for acquisition of knowledge to make money, because there are principles to learn. If it is true that people donate their parents, brothers, sisters, relations friends and wives/husbands to make money. What makes you think that such donors will not be donated by others one day?

The problem is that our people tell us how they sat at the back seat of the car without telling us what transpired while they were seated.

HONOUR FOR ALL:
Though this book is about honour and care for parents, there is need to draw attention to the fact that respect, acknowledgment or reverence does not belong to our parents only. Let us strive to honour all men and women. For the society to be a better place for all, we must demonstrate an understanding that we owe each other honour and care.

The Almighty God commands us to honour all men who deserve honour. Our love for each other should propel us to acknowledge one another in honour. The lack of honour for fellow men and women is responsible for cheap valuation of humans in the society.

HONOUR TEACHERS: It is recommended that we honour those who spend their time in impacting others. Teachers are very important to the project of total emancipation of the total man. Students, protégés, apprentices and all men and women under tutelage are required to honour their teachers and masters.
Teachers communicate knowledge and they deserve

honour. Teachers who respect their calling to lift up mankind out of illiteracy deserve honour. Teachers who respect themselves deserve reciprocal respect and honour from their students.

Let him that is taught in the word communicate unto him that teacheth in all good things.

Galatians 6:6

Though all teachers are not pastors, I consider the fact that they also teach the word. Their ability to interpret the word properly, be it scientific, social, economic or financial affects the society positively and they should be honoured. It is not out of order for parents of those being instructed by teachers to occasionally appreciate the teachers on behalf of their children.

HONOUR KINGS: One of the things kings desire and deserve is honour. Some of them even attempt to demand worship which God is against. However, God requires us to honour kings. Infact, honour for kings is seen as one of the ways to ensure that we live peacefully in all Godliness.

Though God commands that we first pray for kings and those in authority, but most of the kings prefer honour to prayers. Kings consider honour as one of the things which belong to Ceaser, and they believe that they represent Ceaser to their domain.

"And He said unto them, render therefore unto Ceaser the things which be Ceasar's, and unto God the things which be God's".

Luke 20:25

God is Happy when we honour and pray for our kings, but He is displeased when we attempt to worship them. God only should be worshipped.

HONOUR THE QUEEN: Remember that whenever a woman is on the throne, she is addressed as a queen. She should be honoured the same way the king is honoured.

HONOUR THOSE IN AUTHORITY: God expects us to honour and obey those in authority. Under normal circumstances, men and women have the fear of God, live in the fear of God, and recognize God as the final authority from whom their authority flows. All authorities are supposed to be inherited from God. But today, we have authorities that claim to be self-existent.

It is advisable not to resist authorities, so as not to oppose God who is supposed to have put them there. The law has nothing to do against anybody that is law abiding and of good behaviour, but those who are evil and express lawlessness in their behaviour.

You have nothing to fear of any authority, if you are of good behaviour. Infact, if you continually do good, you will earn the commendation of those in authority. Fear God.

RESPECT FOR ALL: The society will not run peacefully if we fail to acknowledge and respect one another. Every one of us owe honour to each other. It is our lack of honour for all that leads to breakdown of law and order in the public and private domain.

Respect they say is reciprocal. Respect attracts respect in return. Honour attracts honour in return. Dishonour attracts dishonour in return. Let us form the habit of honouring one another.

Don't go about demanding respect or honour. Do your best to command respect or honour by offering honour to others first. While, you look forward to honour from others reach out to them first in honour.

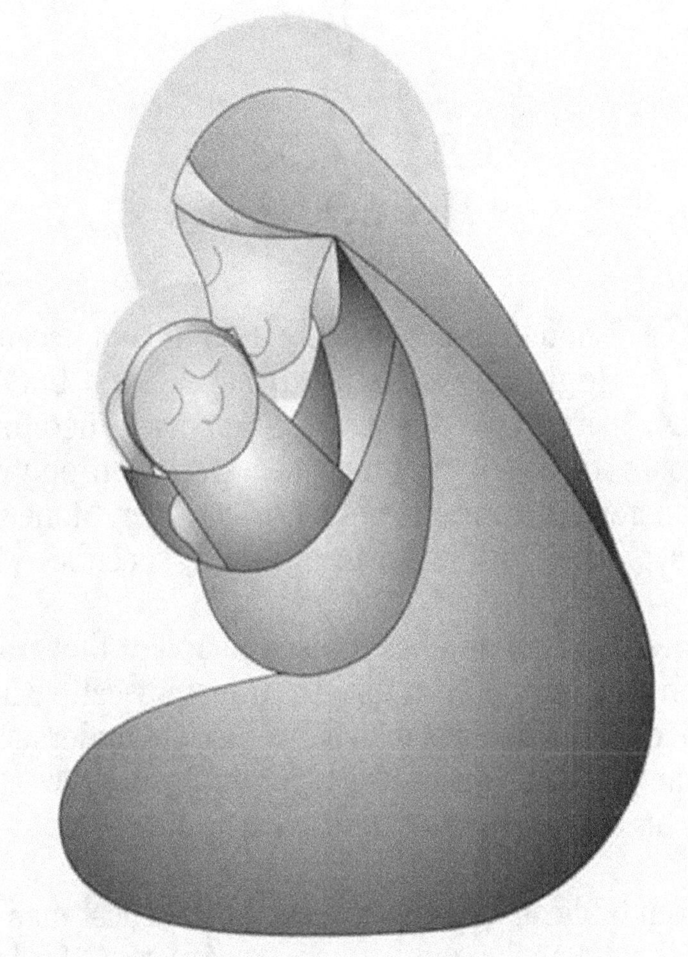

What a caring mother.
Remember her love and care.

8

GIVE BACK TO
THE SOCIETY

Though money is a creation of God because He gives us the ability to make wealth, but the currency is an earthly paper. Therefore, money does not return to heaven, it can only be transferred from one person to another. Money is just a yardstick for measuring earthly success.

However, mankind has refused to accept that truth and has continually refused to transfer wealth while alive. Unfortunately, man has refused to understand that there is no guarantee of continuity of his wealth by his children or his estate when he dies.

From biblical Solomon to Arkad the richest man in the old Babylon and others in America, Jordan, Kuwait, Saudi Arabia, Europe, Africa or what have you, no one has successfully transferred his position of being the richest man on earth to his son or daughter after him.

There is no record to confirm that king Solomon's son or daughter became the next wealthiest person after his demise.

Same is true of all the world's wealthiest men and women before now.

THE TRUTH: One day, the wealthiest men and women in the world will cease to be the wealthiest either by reason of death or earthly business miscalculations in decision making.

However, it is not guaranteed that any of their sons or daughters will replace them in the world as the wealthiest person on earth.

WHAT TO DO: Now that you know that you will not remain world's wealthiest when you die.

The best for you to do is to multiply your wealth by transferring it while you are here on earth. How?

RAISE MORE WEALTHY MEN AND WOMEN: It is regrettable that wealthy men and women have refused to create more wealth for their countries and continents by freeing slaves and employees.

Having a few billionaires in each country is not enough to grow the economy of any nation, because the prosperity of every nation depends on the personal prosperity of each of her citizens or individuals, the more of them we have in any nation, the better for that nation's economy.

Having one man as king with five jets and unused bank balances does not grow a nation's economy. Keeping employees and slaves that are qualified to be freed is not economic growth. If you want to remain the world's richest or wealthiest man or woman while you are here, get out of norms and fear of competition and divide your wealth among faithful men and women and watch them compete with you here on earth.

Alternatively, admit them as partners by diluting ownership of your organization, so on your way out, you can be sure that your protégés are ready already, to step into your shoes.

Inability of business men and women to raise more of their kind in entrepreneurship and competition is one of the major reasons why nations are poor. Standing alone as a capitalist endangers the economy of the nations. Raise more people by giving them interest free startup capital on agreement and accept competition in your line of business.

Establish platforms for people that have faithfully served you over the years to be rewarded. Guide them to recover your investment and offload your supervision and financial interest in their business.

FAMILIES SHOULD RAISE HEIRS TO TAKE OVER:

Every family should strive to raise successful people through the instrument of empowerment. That is the only way to ensure generational wealth creation, transfer and permanent defeat of generational slavery and poverty.

It is dangerous to have one successful person in a family. it is better, stronger and rewarding to raise more successful hands in every family, than have one capitalist there. Empowerment of more people is the answer.

BUILD OLD PEOPLE'S HOME: Do your best to build old people's home where you and others can retire to relax at old age.

SUPPORT ORPHANAGES: Help develop orphanages and health care centres where orphans and the less privileged people can be raised.

Empower people to rise to your status routinely. If you are a millionaire raise millionaires, if you are a billionaire raise billionaires. Be kind to draw as many people as possible as you go up. Your community and environment should feel your presence and impact financially, socialy, spiritually and otherwise.

Your net-worth at exit point from earth should consist of your Balance Sheet and how many people you empowered while you were alive. There should be many of you in your area who have been empowered by you to emulate your footsteps in business.

It is better to multiply yourself while alive, than to pile up your wealth for unknown and uninterested persons at death. Think! Think! Think!

At old age they need your love and care.
A greater percentage of our elderly population are abandoned
or totally disregarded. One day we will get there.
Is this how we wish to be abandoned or disregarded?
The elderly deserve to be honoured, cared for
and highly respected.

9

ROYALTY

A sum paid or payable to a patentee for the use of a patent, an author or composer for each copy of a book sold, or for each public performance of a music, is known as royalty. People of a royal blood or status, heads of a lineage, family or highly regarded members of a family are also referred to as royalties.

A close look at the above definitions will reveal that honour and care for parents, could stand as royalties you offer to parents for cooperating with God in bringing you to earth, contributions to raising you in royalty and highly esteemed status. God chose your parents, as channel that brought you to planet earth.

Children who honour and care for parents extend their royal lineage. By their positive actions, the status of their lineages, families are extended and greatly acknowledged.

YOU ARE A PART OF YOUR PARENTS' PENSION SCHEME.

With the emergence of social media platforms and their attendant social ills, some theorists have tried to push some dirty stuffs suggesting that children should not care for parents at old age. That's a false theory and cannot hold water. For instance, here in Africa, parents do not tie the educational development of children on their children's neck, as it is done in some parts of the world, where students are given refundable college loan that weigh heavily on their shoulders as they begin life.

In Africa some parents pledge, sell their properties, or obtain staff loan in their work places to develop their children or wards. The path of honour requires that you help such parents, when things change for you, to redeem the pledged lands, buy new properties if possible, to replace the disposed ones and assist in ensuring that they are debt-free,on retirement.

Even in the rest of the world, when the burden of college loan is tied on the neck of the child, he or she knew what happened, because most of those parents/guardians, could not afford a loan-free college education.

Truth is that the financial state of parents, has Little or nothing to do with honour and care for them. You owe them honour and care. However, the author does not in anyway, suggest that parents should ignore the need for investments, savings for the rainy days in life, to forestall pains and unnecessary discomfort at old age.

In most cases some parents invest their lifetime earnings to train or develop their children with hope that they will honour and care for them later in life. In some cases, this expectation has ended up a hoax. There are parents who invest as much as twenty million Naira and above to train a child. That figure excludes other cost centres involved in training the child.

If parents invest twenty million Naira at the age of 40 years when most people send their children to higher institution, at sixty-five or seventy years when they retire, there should be something reasonable to face retirement in their personal pension fund, in any of the pension trust companies. Consider also, that at the end of the day, the estate of such parents is left behind for those children who may or may not have honoured and cared for them, while they were alive.

If you truly want to appreciate the investment your parent made in you by way of education, please pause, ask yourself, what is the difference between me and the other child introduced to street begging as a means of livelihood? That fellow had equal birth that was celebrated, but no one took responsibility to invest in his or her life, thereby, leaving the child grow up with mental poverty which is the worst kind of poverty.

The Chief Executive Officers you have in organizations, Scientists, and other respected professionals across the globe, are products of parental empowerment. Though some children invested in their personal development, but before then, someone showed them the way to school.

REMEMBER:

As the curtain for this book work closes, remember that your parents are labouring together, each maintaining his or her division. Your father has the seed but he has no ovum where he can plant the seed. Your mother provides her ovum, receives the seed and incubates the seed until delivery. The seed and the ovum are of equal importance. Though the owner of the seed sometimes, try to claim superiority over the owner of the ovum, truth is that his seed is useless, as long as it cannot be multiplied as commanded by God. Do your best to love them equally.

Your mother is always by your side with so much affection. She gives you a gentle bath, breastfeed you, then proceed to rocking your cradle until you stop crying and close your eyes to sleep. On the other hand, your father loves you so much but without emotional expression on his eyes. He is always on the move in search of daily bread for the family. He seldom sleeps.

Your mother unarguably introduces you to the world, but it is your father that introduces the world to you. While mom boosts of giving life, dad gives living. Your mother ensures that you do not starve by preparing your meals on time, while your father teaches you the value of starvation in order to overcome laziness, the two are of equal importance.

When you remember your mom for being care personified, remember your dad for being responsibility personified. When you talk of mom protecting you from a fall, talk of dad who saves you from remaining on the floor when you fall. He teaches you to get up. Whereas your mom taught you how to walk the first time on earth, it was your dad that taught you the walk of life and its challenges.

Mother tells you to learn by observing her pitfalls in life, while father says,venture and learn from your own experiences. While you thank your mother for reflecting an ideology, you should also thank your father who reflects the reality of living. Whereas a mother's love is known, appreciated by all from childhood, some sons may not know and fully appreciate their father's love towards them, until they become fathers themselves. Why wait till you become a parent, before you know and appreciate, the love of your parents towards you? What a wonderful world. Honour and care for parents.

Remember to celebrate your parents when it is well with you. Here is a good example.

Above: Ex. Gov. Emeka Ihedioha walk on the honour path with his mother
Dame Dorothy Nsonma Ihedioha

Stop The Stopper
Simeon Meremoth

God's plan for placing you on earth is to have dominion, walk in authority, power and prosperity of body, soul; and spirit.

If for any reason you are living beneath your kingdom entitlements, pleading for the crumbs to fall from the table, then you must know that destiny stoppers and destroyers are at work.

Whatever or whoever the devil uses to rob you of your faithful inheritance of living in dominion is a stopper and destroyer of your destiny. This book will help you rediscover and recover your destiny. The author has also taken time to expose key destiny destroyers and stoppers.

This book will serve as a voice of challenge, direction and liberation to as many as are tired of eating the crumbs from the table.

Now is the best time to stop the stopper before he stops you.

The super student
Simeon Meremoth

Man is made to conquer and dominate his environment. But often we are limited by what we think we are not and cannot do or we are simply distracted by things that lead to nowhere.

Great achievers think and believe they can. They know the supernatural power in them and they take appropriate steps towards harnessing those potentials. The first step begins by being a super student.

Honour and care for the man of God
Simeon Meremoth

This book is by Dr Simeon Meremoth is a determined war against dishonour and carelessness about men and women of God in the body of Christ. The book is a must for every person who desires to remain blessed and favoured by God.

You will be exposed to: ***The man of God. *Honour the man or woman of God. *Why you should honour the man or woman of God. *Ways to honour the man or woman of God. *The power of works in the Kingdom. *Benefits of honouring the man or woman of God. *Barriers to recognizing the man or woman of God. *How to care for the man or woman of God. *The minister's health. *Ministerial relationship.**

(Available on hard cover & paper back)

Overtake and be at the top
Simeon Meremoth

Life is a journey. What you make out of it is entirely your choice. The choices you make determine how far you can go. Not in terms of space or time, but in terms of how much you can accomplish. In this book, Simeon Meremoth takes you through the routes great achievers have followed to arrive at the top. You too can overtake and be at the top.

But if you are contented with where you are, or afraid to be lifted to the top, read no further, for you are about to experience a dramatic upliftment in your life.

The Principle of Firstfruits
Simeon Meremoth

In this wonder book, you will discover the secret of overwhelming blessings of God, experience a total turn around in your quest for abundant life, as you understand the full meaning of Firstfruits and align yourself with what God has for you. Find out how the application of the principle of Firstfruits is designed to abundantly bless you.

**The Power of Generational Blessings
Simeon Meremoth**

Enough of the curses. Start blessing your sons and daughters.